Destinations 2
Grammar for Academic Success

Nancy Herzfeld-Pipkin
GROSSMONT COLLEGE

THOMSON
™
HEINLE

Australia • Canada • Singapore • Spain • United Kingdom • United States

THOMSON

™

HEINLE

Destinations 2: Grammar for Academic Success
Nancy Herzfeld-Pipkin

Publisher, Academic ESL: *James W. Brown*
Director of Content Development: *Anita Raducanu*
Director of Product Marketing: *Amy Mabley*
Executive Marketing Manager: *Jim McDonough*
Senior Field Marketing Manager: *Donna Lee Kennedy*
Editorial Assistant: *Katherine Reilly*

Cover Image: © *Getty Images/RubberBall Productions/RF*

Sr. Production Editor: *Maryellen Eschmann-Killeen*
Sr. Print Buyer: *Mary Beth Hennebury*
Development Editor: *Sarah Barnicle*
Production Project Manager: *Chrystie Hopkins*
Production Services: *Nesbitt Graphics, Inc.*
Compositor: *Parkwood Composition Services*
Cover Designer: *Gina Petti/Rotunda Design House*
Printer: *The West Group*

For permission to use material from this text or product,
submit a request online at http://www.thomsonrights.com

Any additional questions about permissions can be
submitted by email to thomsonrights@thomson.com

ISBN 10: 1-4130-2245-6
ISBN 13: 978-1-4130-2245-2

For more information contact Thomson Heinle,
25 Thomson Place, Boston, Massachusetts 02210 USA,
or you can visit our Internet site at
http://elt.thomson.com

Credits appear on page 273, which constitutes a
continuation of the copyright page.

To the Teacher

Destinations 2: Grammar for Academic Success was written to provide students a full range of grammar practice at the high intermediate level. By incorporating unit themes, contexts, and vocabulary from its companion book *Destinations 2: Writing for Academic Success,* the *Destinations* grammar workbook is designed to be used as a supplementary text in writing courses or as the grammar text in linked writing and grammar courses.

LINKS TO *DESTINATIONS 2:* WRITING FOR ACADEMIC SUCCESS

- Grammar points covered in each unit will be especially useful in student writing assignments of the writing text. Grammar topics were chosen with the writing assignments in mind.
- Examples of sentence combining techniques taught in the writing book also appear in the corresponding units of the grammar workbook.
- Vocabulary from the writing book is recycled in the grammar lessons of the corresponding units.
- The materials in the grammar workbook closely follow the order of the same thematic material introduced in the writing book. That is, the grammar points at the beginning of a unit follow the information or topics presented at the beginning of the corresponding writing unit. In the same way, the topics that are presented at the end of the writing book unit are presented at the end of the grammar book unit as well.
- Some exercises and activities expound on the topics introduced in the writing book. Other topics may be somewhat different from information presented in the writing book, but they are always closely related.

OVERVIEW OF UNITS

Each of the six units in the grammar workbook corresponds to a unit in the *Destinations 2* writing text. Each grammar unit contains five to seven lessons; each of the 36 lessons covers one grammar point or sometimes two related grammar points. In addition, in three places topics are introduced with general information either before a unit or within one as follows:

1. Introduction to Verbs and Auxiliaries serves to introduce material in Units One and Two.
2. Introduction to Modals serves to introduce Unit Three.
3. Introduction to Prepositions serves to introduce three lessons in Unit Five.

OVERVIEW OF LESSONS

• Each lesson provides a variety of activities/exercises in order to afford students many opportunities to practice and participate. Due to the variations in time and purpose of individual classes, it is not necessarily expected that every teacher will cover everything in each lesson. Teachers should feel free to choose those activities that best suit the needs and abilities of their particular students.

• Many of the exercises in this book have more than one possible answer.

  1. In some of the more structured activities, the directions explicitly tell students that more than one answer may be appropriate.

  2. In the less structured exercises many answers are possible. These exercises have been included to show students that several variations may be acceptable. It is hoped this approach will help them when dealing with English outside the classroom where they may encounter such variations. It is also hoped that this approach will help students comfortably use and manipulate the language.

PRESENTATION OF LESSONS

Each lesson presents a grammar topic and provides practice with the grammar in the following ways:

  1. *Photo or illustration with example sentences*
  The photo or illustration reviews or relates to a topic in the *Destinations* writing text. The accompanying example sentences introduce the grammar and often include recycled vocabulary or ideas from the writing text.

  2. *Questions*
  The questions ask students to focus on the grammar of the lesson by analyzing specific parts of the example sentences. This section is meant as an inductive exercise for students to figure out (or state as review) the grammar point.

  3. *Explanation*
  This section provides rules, charts, and discussion of the grammatical focus of the lesson. This is the only part of the lesson that does not ask students to complete a task.

  4. *Practice*
  Each lesson begins with controlled exercises. These exercises ask students to fill in the blanks, complete matching activities, answer true or false questions about given sentences, or choose the correct form. Every lesson also presents an error correction or editing exercise that asks students to find the mistakes and correct them.

  Each lesson also has some activities that ask students to be more creative and independent. In all of these activities, students must use the particular grammatical structure from the lesson as much as possible. Some activities ask students to complete sentences using given words or information. Others ask students to create their own sentences based on specific situations or information. These activities often afford students an opportunity to write about topics related to those they may write about for assignments in the *Destinations 2* writing text.

Although all the exercises in the text can be used as pair or group work, the exercises that would work especially well in groups are marked with the group icon, which is also found in the writing text. Many exercise directions make suggestions for pair work and class work.

Marked by this icon, references to *Destinations 2: Writing for Academic Success* have been made throughout the grammar text's explanations and exercises. There are numerous suggestions for review of topics such as coordinating and subordinating conjunctions as well as sentence combining techniques. The writing examples students encounter in the grammar workbook will reinforce many of the concepts learned in the writing text.

APPENDICES

The appendices include reference information such as lists of irregular verb forms, verbs followed by gerunds or infinitives, and spelling rules governing verbs and nouns. Students are reminded to refer to this information in related lessons.

Contents

INTRODUCTION TO VERBS AND AUXILIARIES

About Verbs

The following is a general review of verbs before you study more specific information about verbs and verb tenses.

A) What is a verb?

Do you think a verb is an action word? Many verbs do show action, but not all verbs are action words. Look at the following list of words. Put a line under the verbs. Circle the words that show action.

> jump   believe   earthquake   understand   tornado   speak

B) What grammatical change can these words make that most other words cannot?

Verbs can change with the time. This means verbs have different endings, such as *-s, -ed, -ing*.

C) Do verbs always have these endings?

No. English verbs and verb tenses can be confusing because sometimes, but not always, we use these endings.

> **EXAMPLE:**   I jump   you jump   she/he/it jump<u>s</u>   we jump   they jump

Remember: In English verbs *can* have different endings, but this does not mean that all verbs will always have an ending.

D) Does a verb always indicate the time of a sentence?

No. Be careful not to trust a verb to tell you the time because verbs can be unreliable. Look at the following sentence. What is the time?

> *He is playing soccer at the park on 15th Street.*

1. The time in this sentence might be *right now.* Your friend is not home, and you are asking his mother where he is. This is her answer.
2. The time in this sentence might also be *future.* You ask your friend's mother what your friend's weekend plans are, and this sentence is her answer.

E) If you cannot always rely on verbs to indicate the time, how can you know the time in a sentence?

You must carefully look at the situation or context to know the time. In addition, you should look for *time words* that give more information about the time. Verbs and time words can work together to give you a better understanding of the time.

> **EXAMPLES:**
>
> Where is Bob? He is playing soccer at the park on 15th Street **right now**.
>
> What is Bob doing **next Saturday**? He is playing soccer at the park on 15th Street.

About Auxiliaries

What is an auxiliary?

An auxiliary is a word that works with a verb. Some people call these words *helping verbs*.

Auxiliaries in English:

A. *be   have   do*

These words often work with the main verb of a sentence. They may be necessary for grammar, and these may change with time.

> **EXAMPLES:**   We **are** reading this information right now.
>   auxiliary verb
>
> We **were** reading this information at 10 PM last night.
>   auxiliary   verb

Units One and Two will discuss many ways to use these three auxiliaries with main verbs.

B. *can   could   should   may   might   will   would   must   shall*

The above words are called *modals*. They add meaning to a sentence. You will learn more about the grammar and meaning of modals in Unit 3 of this book.

> **EXAMPLES:**   You **should** study this page carefully.
>   auxiliary   verb
>
> You **will** need to know this information.
>   auxiliary verb

Past Time

Simple Past and Used To

[1]The professor **lectured** for two full hours and **did not stop** for questions. [2]Nothing **distracted** her. [3]Some students **thought** about taking a nap. [4]**Did** anyone **listen** to the entire lecture?

Presentation 1

Questions

1. Look at the verbs in bold that are not negative in sentences 1 and 2. What is the time of these verbs? How do you know this? How is the verb in bold in sentence 3 different from the verb in sentence 2?

2. Look at the negative verb in sentence 1. What is the rule for making a negative sentence?

3. Look at the question in sentence 4. What is the rule for making a question?

Explanation—Simple Past

1. **Regular verbs: verb + *ed***

   Nothing *distracted* the professor. She *talked* for a long time.

2. **Verbs with spelling changes** (See Appendix G for rules.)

   The professor *lectured* for a full hour. She *stopped* at the end of the class.

3. **Irregular verbs: various endings** (See Appendix A for list of verbs.)

   The professor *spoke* about many things. Some students *thought* about taking a nap.

4. **Time words often found with past tense verbs:**

yesterday   ago (three days ago/long ago)

last week/month/year   a specific year (1983)

5. **Negative sentences**

RULE: Add the word *not* after the auxiliary. The simple past in English is usually a one-word verb that does not have an auxiliary. Therefore, we add *did* (past of auxiliary *do*) + *not* for negative sentences.

The professor *did not (didn't*) stop* for questions. Some students *did not (didn't*) take* notes.

Do not add the *-ed* ending to the verb. The auxiliary *did* is already in the past, and you do not need to indicate past again.

Follow this pattern for negative sentences with past tense verbs:

subject	auxiliary	not	verb (simple form)	
The professor	did	not	stop	for questions.
Some students	did	not	take	notes.

6. **Questions**

a. **Yes/no questions**

RULE: Place the auxiliary to the left of the subject of the sentence. As in the case of negative sentences, add *did* (past of auxiliary *do*) for questions. Do not add the *-ed* ending to the verb. The auxiliary *did* is already in the past, and you do not need it again.

Did the professor *stop* for questions?

Follow this pattern for yes/no questions with past tense verbs:

auxiliary	subject	verb (simple form)	
Did	the professor	stop	for questions?
Did	some students	take	notes?

b. **Question word questions**

Add the question word and place the auxiliary *did* to the left of the subject to make the sentence a question.

When did the professor stop for questions? *Why did* some students *take* notes?

---

*Contractions are often used in conversation. They are not usually used in formal writing.

Follow this pattern for question word questions with past tense verbs:

question word	auxiliary	subject	verb (simple form)	
When	did	the professor	stop	for questions?
Why	did	some students	take	notes?
			verb (simple past)	
*Who			gave	the lecture?
*What			distracted	the professor?

*Note: When the question word replaces the subject, do not use the auxiliary *did*. Follow the usual word order of the statement.

7. Negatives and questions with *be* as the main verb in the sentence

   a. When a form of *be* is the main verb in a sentence in past time (*was* or *were*), do not add the auxiliary *did*.
   b. For a negative sentence, add the *not* after *was* or *were*.

   The professor's lecture *was not (wasn't[†])* too long.

   c. For a question, move the *was/were* to the left of the subject.

   Was the professor's lecture too long? *Why was* the professor's lecture too long?

Practice

Activity 1

Fill in the spaces in the paragraph with the correct past form of the verb in parentheses.

A. I always (know) _____ that I (have) _____ a visual
    ₁ ... learning style. In elementary school I (memorize) _____
    my multiplication tables by seeing them in my mind. My best

    friend (be) _____ a tactile/kinesthetic learner, and she

    (learn) _____ best through hands-on activities. We both

    (be—negative) _____ very good auditory learners.

B. John (have—negative) _____ an easy time in his communications

    class last year. He (know—negative) _____ the course would

    include class discussions when he (register) _____ for it. He

    (think) _____ the group work (be) _____ difficult to

_____
†Contractions are often used in conversation. They are not usually used in formal writing.

follow, especially because his group (include) _____ mostly
                                                    6
native speakers of English. He (learn) _____ a lot in the class,
                                              7
though.

C. Last semester my friend's philosophy class (be) _____ very
                                                          1
difficult for her because she (understand—negative) _____ the
                                                            2
professor's lectures very well. She (decide) _____ to find out
                                                   3
more about her learning style. She (find) _____ some
                                                4
information on the Internet about the three different styles: auditory,
visual, and tactile/kinesthetic. From this information she (realize)
_____ her style was visual. This (mean) _____ her
         5   6
learning style (match—negative) _____ the teaching style of
                                        7
the professor.

Activity 2

*The following conversation is between a student and his counselor. Find seven
mistakes and show how to correct them. The first mistake is an example.*

Counselor: Good morning, Rob. It's nice to see you again. I ~~seed~~ *saw* you
             just a few weeks ago. Were you have a special reason to make
             this appointment to see me?

Rob: Yes. I signed up for the chemistry class that we talk about last
             semester, but maybe it was a mistake.

Counselor: A mistake? Did something happened to make you think that?

Rob: Well, the first few classes gived me trouble. I no had a prob-
             lem in the lab classes, just the lecture ones.

Counselor: Maybe you are a more tactile/kinesthetic learner. We did talk
             about how to employ new strategies to help you with this
             kind of problem?

Rob: We started to discuss that, but we stoped because of time.
             Can you give me some suggestions about how to study more
             efficiently or help me with this particular class?

Activity 3

Rewrite each of the following sentences in three ways as follows:

(a) Write a negative sentence, (b) write a yes/no question, and (c) write a question word question using the word given.

1. Laura took a very interesting child development class last semester.

    a. _____

    b. _____

    c. (where) _____

2. She enjoyed listening to the instructor's lectures every class.

    a. _____

    b. _____

    c. (why) _____

3. She used a lot of body language to make the lectures interesting.

    a. _____

    b. _____

    c. (how) _____

Presentation 2—*Used To*

Read the example, the questions, and the explanation that follow.

> Sarah **used to** enjoy her lecture classes every semester, but she **didn't use to** enjoy her lab classes. She realized she is an auditory learner, so the lecture classes were easier for her.

Questions

1. What does the expression *used to* say about the past? Do you see any endings on or changes to the verbs that follow this expression?

2. What change do you see on the negative form of this expression?

Explanation—*Used To*

1. *Used to*   Sarah *used to* enjoy only her lecture classes. These days she enjoys her lab classes as well.

    The expression *used to* means something was done in the past on a regular basis, but it finished and is not done anymore. It may also show contrast between the past and the present. Do not add an ending or change the verb that follows *used to*.

2. **Negative with *used to*** She *did not (didn't*) use to enjoy* her lab classes.

Add the auxiliary *did* and place the word *not* before *used to*. Then make a spelling change with the expression *used to: change "used" to "use."* Do not add an ending to the verb.

subject	auxiliary	not	*used to* + verb	
She	did	not	use to enjoy	her lab classes

3. **Questions with *used to***

Place the auxiliary *did* to the left of the subject. Then make a spelling change with the expression *used to: change "used" to "use."* Do not add an ending to the verb.

auxiliary	subject	*used to* + verb	
Did	Sarah	use to enjoy	her lab classes?

For question word questions, add the question word and place the auxiliary *did* to the left of the subject to make the sentence a question. Then make a spelling change with the expression *used to: change "used" to "use."* Do not add an ending to the verb.

question word	auxiliary	subject	*used to* + verb	
Why	did	Sarah	use to enjoy	only some classes?

Activity 4

Complete the paragraph below with the past tense of one of the following verbs. Add used to and/or make the sentence negative where indicated. Some verbs may fit in more than one space, but you should use each verb only one time.

worry	become	get	perceive
take	feel	be	score

Joe (used to) _____ nervous when he _____ standardized
            1   2
tests, such as IQ tests. He (used to) _____ upset because he
                                                  3
_____ that it _____ impossible to study for them. As a
       4   5
result, he (used to—negative) _____ well on them. He (negative)
                                          6
_____ about exams or quizzes in his classes, though. He
       7
_____ those as easier because he could study for them.
       8

---

*Contractions are often used in conversation. They are not usually used in formal writing.

Activity 5

Use the information given to write negative sentences or questions in the past.

EXAMPLES:

(yes/no question)   you / enjoy / taking lab classes

Did you enjoy taking lab classes?

(negative)   I / used to enjoy / long lecture classes.

I didn't use to enjoy long lecture classes.

1. (negative)   the students / participate / in many discussions with the teacher

_____

2. (yes/no question)   you / visualize / something to remember it

_____

3. (question with *why*)   he / enroll / in so many lab classes

_____

4. (negative)   people / used to / understand / about learning styles

_____

5. (yes/no question)   people / used to / try / to test / intelligence

_____

6. (question with *how*)   people / used to / test / intelligence

_____

Activity 6   *(Review coordinating conjunctions: Unit One, pages 8–13.)*

A. *Complete the following sentences in the past tense according to your personal experiences.*

1. My favorite class as a child _____

2. I liked this class best, for _____

3. My teacher in that class _____

4. In that class I used to _____

5. In that class I didn't use to _____

6. The class fit my learning style, so _____

B. *Think about a class that was difficult for you in the past. Answer the following questions with complete sentences about the class. Try to include* used to *in at least one of your answers.*

1. Which class was the most difficult for you?

   _____

2. When and where did you take that class?

   _____

3. What particular part of that class was the most difficult and why?

   _____

4. What did you use to do when you had problems with that class? How did you deal with the problem(s) in that class?

   _____

5. Was your learning style related in any way to the reason you didn't enjoy or were not successful in that class?

   _____

General/Habitual Time

Simple Present

[1]Jenna always **tries** to tape her professor's lectures as a study strategy. [2]She usually **studies** by listening to the lectures again. [3]She often **does not understand** her notes when she **reads** them without the auditory explanations.

Presentation

Questions

1. What is the time in the sentences of this caption? What information can you learn about the time from the verbs in bold? Do any other words in these sentences give you information about the time?

2. Look at the negative verb in the last sentence. What is the rule for making a negative sentence?

Explanation—Simple Present

1. **Verb or verb + -s** Add the -s ending only when the subject is she/he/it or a single item (third person singular).

   She *understands* it without the auditory explanations. We *understand* it with the auditory explanations.

2. **Verbs with spelling changes** (See Appendix G for rules.)

   She usually *studies* by listening to the lectures again. He always *goes* to class on time.

3. Use these verb forms for things people do regularly or as a routine, such as habits and customs. Use them also to talk about scientific facts. The time in these sentences is **general** or **habitual** time. It is not "present time" (or right now).

4. Time words that usually indicate general or habitual time. Another name for these words is *frequency words* or *frequency adverbs*.

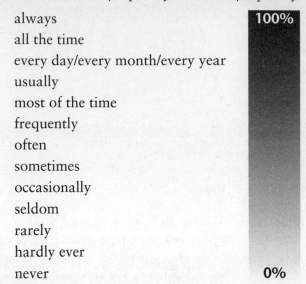

always	100%
all the time	
every day/every month/every year	
usually	
most of the time	
frequently	
often	
sometimes	
occasionally	
seldom	
rarely	
hardly ever	
never	0%

These words usually go between the subject and the verb of the sentence. Sometimes you will find these words at the beginning or end of a sentence.

She *always tries* to tape the professor's lectures. She tapes the lectures *all the time.*

5. **Negative sentences**

RULE: Add the word *not* after the auxiliary. The simple present in English is usually a one-word verb that does not have an auxiliary. Therefore, we add *do* or *does* (depending on the subject) + *not* to make it negative.

She often *does not (doesn't*) understand* the material.
We *do not (don't*) understand* the material.

Do not add the *-s* ending to the verb when you use *does.*

Follow this pattern for negative sentences in general or habitual time:

subject	auxiliary	not	verb (simple form)	
She	does	not	understand	the material.
We	do	not	understand	the material.

6. **Questions**

a. **Yes/no questions**

RULE: Place the auxiliary to the left of the subject of the sentence. As in the case of negative sentences, add *do* or *does* for questions.

Does she *understand* the material? *Do* other students *understand* it?

Do not add the *-s* ending.

---

*Contractions are often used in conversation. They are not usually used in formal writing.

Follow this pattern for yes/no questions in general/habitual time:

auxiliary	subject	verb (simple form)	
Does	she	understand	the material?
Do	the other students	understand	it?

b. **Question word questions**

Add the question word and place the auxiliary *do/does* to the left of the subject to make the sentence a question. After you add these words, do not add the *-s* ending to the verb.

> *Why does* she always *tape* the lectures? *Why do* students *tape* the lectures?

Follow this pattern for question word questions in general/habitual time:

question word	auxiliary	subject	verb (simple form)	
Why	does	she	tape	the lectures?
Why	do	students	tape	the lectures?
			verb (simple present)	
Who*			tapes	the lectures?
What*			helps	her understand?

*Note: When the question word replaces the subject, do not use the auxiliary *do/does*. Follow the usual word order of the sentence.

7. Negatives and questions with *be* as a main verb in the sentence

When a form of *be* is the main verb in a sentence in general/habitual time *(am/is/are)*, do not add the auxiliary *do* or *does*.

For a negative sentence, add the *not* after *am/is/are*.

> The professor's lecture *is not (isn't†)* easy to understand.

For a question, place the *am/is/are* to the left of the subject.

> *Is* the professor's lecture easy to understand? *Why is* the professor's lecture difficult for her?

---

†Contractions are often used in conversation. They are not usually used in formal writing.

Practice

Activity 1   *(Review coordinating conjunctions: Unit One, pages 8–13.)*

Fill in the blank lines to show general/habitual time.

A. Jenna (be) _____ an auditory learner. She always (listen)
1
_____ to the radio, but she rarely (read) _____ a
2   3
newspaper for the news. She sometimes (use) _____ jingles to
4
learn things, and she especially (enjoy) _____ a discussion
5
format for her classes. She (work—negative) _____ efficiently in
6
a hands-on class.

B. Marc and Ellen (be) _____ twins, and they often (follow)
1
_____ the same learning strategies in school. They
2
(like—negative) _____ noisy distractions when they (study)
3
_____ , so they often (go) _____ to the library to
4   5
work. They also frequently (draw) _____ charts and diagrams
6
to remember new material, but they (take—negative) _____
7
many hands-on lab classes. They (be—negative) _____ very
8
good at manipulating things or taking things apart and putting them
back together with their hands.

Activity 2   *(Review coordinating conjunctions: Unit One, pages 8–13.)*

Bill is an auditory learner, Ann is a tactile/kinesthetic learner, and Dara is a visual learner. Read about how each one learns or does things, and complete the opposite information about the others by filling in the blanks. Follow the example given.

EXAMPLE:
Ann enjoys using tools to make things. Dara *doesn't enjoy* using tools.

1. Ann likes to paint with oil and water colors. Bill _____ to paint
    at all.

2. Ann prefers hands-on activities. Bill and Dana _____
    a
    hands-on activities. They _____ to watch demonstrations.
    b

3. Ann is good at finding her way around. Bill _____ at finding his way around.

4. Drawing pictures helps Dara remember things. Drawing pictures

   _____ Ann remember things.

5. Bill and Ann are not skillful at making charts or maps. Dara

   _____ skillful at making them.

6. Dara learns best through visual presentations. Bill and Ann _____ best through visual presentations.

7. Dara is a quiet person and doesn't enjoy talking to others. Bill

   _____ a quiet person, and he _____ talking to others.
        a   b

8. Bill uses musical jingles to help him learn things. Ann and Dara

   _____ musical jingles to learn.

9. Ann does not watch television for the news, but she reads a newspaper

   instead. Bill _____ a newspaper to learn the news, so he
                       a

   _____ television.
        b

Activity 3

In the following paragraph find nine mistakes and show how to correct them.

Bob know that his learning style is tactile/kinesthetic. He tries to take as many lab classes or field seminars as possible. His major is geography, and many of those classes involves field work, including trips to parks and nature reserves. For him, those classes is easy and interesting. Some of his friends doesn't understand this. They not are very good at those kinds of classes. They often tells him to take lecture classes with them. Sometimes he gos to those classes also, but he does not takes too many of them. He is happy that his major fits his learning style.

Activity 4

Interview a partner about his/her learning style. Use each of the learning characteristics given to make a question. Write the question and the answer on the lines given.

EXAMPLE:

characteristic: like to talk with hands

Question: Do you like to talk with your hands?

Answer: She/He likes to talk with his hands. OR, She/He does not like

to talk with her/his hands.

> take things apart and put them together
>
> dislike reading from a computer screen
>
> understand and follow maps well
>
> remember information from a whiteboard or chart
>
> enjoy talking to others
>
> feel comfortable doing things but not watching them

1. Question: _____

   Answer: _____

2. Question: _____

   Answer: _____

3. Question: _____

   Answer: _____

4. Question: _____

   Answer: _____

5. Question: _____

   Answer: _____

6. Question: _____

   Answer: _____

Activity 5

Think about some of your past habits or customs in a place you lived before or in a school you attended before. Then think about how you do these things differently now. Write two sentences, one about this custom or habit in the past using used to *and one about how you do it more recently using a frequency word for general/habitual time.*

EXAMPLES:

At my old school I *used to study* only at home. At this school I *often study* in the library.

At my parents' house I *didn't use to* cook for myself. Here I *sometimes cook* my own meals.

1. _____

2. _____

Present Time

Present Progressive (Continuous*)

[1]These students **are taking** a class, but they **are not sitting** in a classroom. [2]They **are studying** in the field today because they **are examining** the unique plants of the area for a biology class. [3]One student **is explaining** the information to another right now.

Presentation

Questions

1. What do you find at the end of each verb in bold? Do you see any other words that work with these verbs?

2. What is the time in these sentences? What information can you learn about the time from the verbs in bold? Are there any other words in these sentences that give you information about the time? Is the action in each of these sentences finished or not finished?

3. Look at the negative verb in the first sentence. What is the rule for making the sentence negative?

Explanation—Present Progressive (Continuous*)

1. **Present progressive = present of auxiliary** *be (am/is/are)* **+ verb +** *-ing*

   Be sure to have all three of these parts, including the *-ing* ending. This ending tells you the action is not finished or is continuous.

   They *are studying* in the field today.
        1   2   3

   One student *is explaining* the information to another right now.
             1   2   3

2. **Verbs with spelling changes** (See Appendix G for rules.)

   These people *are taking* a class, but they *are not sitting* in a classroom. They *are examining* the unique plants of the area.

---

*Note: Sometimes the word *continuous* is used in place of the word *progressive*. These words have the same meaning.

3. Use these verb forms for present time or actions that are taking place now/at the moment. You can also use them to talk about something that is not finished or in progress over a longer period of time (extended present).

   EXAMPLES:

   This month the professor *is working* on a new project.

   This semester we *are studying* grammar.

4. Time words that usually indicate present time:

   now   *right now*   *at the moment*   *at present*   *today*

   Time words that can indicate extended present:

   this week   *this semester*   *this month*   *this year*

5. **Negative sentences**

   RULE: Add the word *not* after the auxiliary to make a sentence negative.

   These students *are not (aren't*) sitting* in a classroom. The professor *is not (isn't*) explaining* the lesson.

   Follow this pattern for negative sentences with present progressive verbs:

subject	auxiliary *(be)*	not	verb + *-ing*	
The professor	is	not	explaining	the lesson.
These students	are	not	sitting	in a classroom.

6. **Questions**

   a. **Yes/no questions**

   RULE: Move the auxiliary to the left of the subject.

   Are the students *studying* in the field? *Is* the professor *explaining* the information?

   Follow this pattern for yes/no questions with present progressive verbs:

auxiliary *(be)*	subject	verb + *-ing*	
Are	the students	studying	in the field?
Is	the professor	explaining	the information?

   b. **Question word questions**

   RULE: Add the question word and move the auxiliary to the left of the subject.

   Why are the students *studying* in the field? *When is* the professor *explaining* the information?

---

*Contractions are often used in conversation. They are not usually used in formal writing.

Follow this pattern for question word questions with present progressive verbs:

question word	auxiliary *(be)*	subject	verb + *-ing*	
Why	are	the students	studying	in the field?
When	is	the professor	explaining	the information?
*Who	is		studying	in the field?
*Which plant	is		growing	here?

*Note: When the question word replaces the subject, follow the usual word order of a statement.

Practice

Activity 1   *(Review coordinating conjunctions: Unit One, pages 8–13.)*

A.   *Fill in the spaces with the correct form of the present progressive of the verbs given.*

Right now some students (prepare) ـــــــــــــــــ for an experiment in
                                          1
their chemistry lab class. The instructor (review) ـــــــــــــــــ the
                                                              2
procedures and (explain) ـــــــــــــــــ some details. Some students
                                      3
(write) ـــــــــــــــــ notes, but others (listen) ـــــــــــــــــ carefully
            4   5
only. One student (draw) ـــــــــــــــــ some diagrams, so he can
                                     6
remember the procedures easily. All of the students (do) ـــــــــــــــــ
                                                                        7
whatever works best for them to be most successful in this class.

B.   *Fill in the spaces below with the correct form of the present progressive of the verbs given. Use each verb only one time.*

move	stop	say	experience	take
give	prepare	talk	help	

This semester Bill ـــــــــــــــــ a math class called Calculus for Business
                                1
Majors. Today he ـــــــــــــــــ some difficulty with the class because the
                              2
teacher ـــــــــــــــــ quickly through the material. She (negative)
                    3
ـــــــــــــــــ for questions and (negative) ـــــــــــــــــ students a
            4   5
chance to review the particularly difficult material in class. All the students
ـــــــــــــــــ about the format of the class and they (negative)
            6
ـــــــــــــــــ good things about it. Today Bill and a friend ـــــــــــــــــ
            7   8
a long homework assignment together, so they ـــــــــــــــــ each other.
                                                                  9

Activity 2   *(Review coordinating conjunctions: Unit One, pages 8–13.)*

In the following student's journal, find six mistakes and show how to correct them.

This week in my communications class everyone are working in groups to make presentations to the class. Today one person is finish the last interviews with people at school about their perceptions of the college experience. Now the others in the group work on the presentation, and they are trying to use everyone's strengths. Right now George is prepares the talk to give because he is a verbal person. Our mathematicians, Amy and Bob, is calculating the results of the interviews to put on posters. Darlene is very artistic, so she are drawing the illustrations and graphs for the posters.

Activity 3

Using the information given under each line below, write questions a counselor might ask a student. Use the present progressive form of the verb in each question. Be sure to use appropriate punctuation as well.

1. _____

   (yes/no question)   you / take / classes to fit / your learning style / this semester

2. _____

   how much time / you / spend / reviewing your notes

3. _____

   (yes/no question)   you / find / ways to adapt your learning style / in your lecture classes

4. _____

   why / you / miss / so many classes this semester

5. _____

   how many / lab classes / register / for this week

Activity 4

Fill in the blanks with the correct form of the verb in parentheses. Use the simple past, the simple present, or the present progressive form of the verb.

This semester I (take) ＿＿＿＿＿＿＿＿ a very interesting environmental
                              1
studies class with a lab section. During the first lab class I (meet)

＿＿＿＿＿＿＿＿ some other students, and we (form) ＿＿＿＿＿＿＿ a study
        2   3
group last month. We (get) ＿＿＿＿＿＿＿ together at a coffee house near
                              4
school once a week. At these meetings we (review) ＿＿＿＿＿＿＿ our
                                                          5
notes and (discuss) ＿＿＿＿＿＿＿ the material. Sometimes one of us
                          6
(bring) ＿＿＿＿＿＿＿ extra information about a particular topic. This week
              7
we (plan) ＿＿＿＿＿＿＿ a longer meeting to study for our big midterm.
                8
I (make) ＿＿＿＿＿＿＿ some charts and illustrations, and another student
              9
(research) ＿＿＿＿＿＿＿ online to bring more information to this
                  10
study session.

Activity 5

Each of the following pictures shows people doing something unusual. Write two complete sentences about these pictures as follows:

a. Describe the action that is unusual using a verb in the present progressive.
b. Describe what someone usually does in this situation using a verb in the simple present.

EXAMPLE:

If the picture shows a firefighter running away from a house on fire, you can say:

a. This firefighter is running away from a burning building.

b. A firefighter doesn't usually run away from a fire.

OR A firefighter usually helps put out a fire.

1.

2.

3.

4.

5.

Stative/Non-Action Verbs

[1]These students **are taking** a difficult exam now. [2]One student **seems** to be uncomfortable. [3]Maybe he **does not understand** the material, or maybe he **has a cold** right now. [4]The other students **don't notice** something is wrong with him.

Presentation

Questions

1. What is the time in this caption? How do you know this? What specific words tell you the time?

2. Why does the verb in sentence 1 have a different ending from the other verbs in this caption?

Explanation—Stative/Non-Action Verbs

1. Some verbs are not usually used in the progressive. These verbs are called *stative* or *non-action* verbs.

    One student *seems* to be uncomfortable right now. Maybe he *has* a cold.

2. The following groups show some common stative verbs:

    emotions: hate, like, love, dislike, fear, trust

    mental states: know, remember, forget, believe/feel, think, understand, suppose, mean

    perceptions and senses: hear, see, smell, taste, notice, appear, seem, sound, look

    needs and preferences: want, need, prefer

    measurements: cost, weigh, contain

    possession: own, possess, belong, have

    For a more complete list, see Appendix B.

3. Some of these verbs can be used either with or without the progressive ending *(-ing),* depending on the meaning. For example:

think: When the meaning is *believe,* and it expresses an opinion, do not use the progressive.

> I *think* this is an interesting class. She *thinks* this class fits her learning style.

When you have ideas in your head, and you are thinking about something, you can use the *-ing* ending.

> I *am thinking* about my difficult lab assignment. He *is thinking* about his music class.

have: When you want to show ownership, do not use the progressive.

> You *have* an old edition of that book. My friend *has* some lab supplies to give me.

When you use specific expressions such as *have a party, have a good time, have a problem,* you can use the *-ing* ending.

> We *are having* a good time in this class. My friend *is having* a problem in that class.

Some other verbs can be used with or without the *-ing* ending as well. Some examples are:

taste: This food *tastes* terrible. I *am tasting* the food to see if it needs salt.

feel: I *feel* sick, but she *feels* happy. I *am feeling* the new table for scratch marks.

weigh: These bananas *weigh* 3 pounds. I *am weighing* the bananas to figure out the price.

smell: The food on the stove *smells* delicious. I *am smelling* the food because I can't eat it yet.

look: You *look* tired today. She *is looking* out the window to watch the rain.

Practice

Activity 1   *(Review coordinating conjunctions: Unit One, pages 8–13.)*

Circle the correct form of the verb in parentheses in a student's two journal entries below.

Monday—January 31

This week in my psychology class we (learn/are learning) about our personal combinations of different kinds of intelligence. We (are studying/study) Gardner's theory, and it (appears/is appearing) to explain some things about my personality and interests. I (think/am thinking) it is a very interesting topic, so I (am wanting/want) to learn more about it now. I still (am not understanding/don't understand) some particular aspects of the theory, so I might try to find some more information on my own.

Tuesday—February 1

Right now I (am taking/take) a break from my Internet search about learning styles and the theory of multiple intelligences. I (feel/am feeling) like I (am enjoying/enjoy) much more about myself now. Now I (am knowing/know) why I (am enjoying/enjoy) my music and art courses so much this semester and why I (prefer/am preferring) to take those classes instead of the more traditional lecture style classes. I (am thinking/think) about making an appointment with my counselor at school to discuss my college plan and my major. I (am/am being) still officially undecided, but this week (seems/is seeming) to be a good time to make a decision.

Activity 2

Lauren and David are preparing a meal in a culinary arts class. Fill in the spaces of their conversation with the correct form of each verb in parentheses. Some of the answers will be negative or in the form of a question.

Lauren: We (need) _____ to get a few more ingredients
                            1
                ready so we can make the next part of the meal.

David: I (think—negative) _____ we (have) _____
                                  2   3
                enough potatoes. I (weigh) _____ them now.
                                            4

Lauren: How much (weigh) _____ they _____ ?
                                      5   6

David: It (look) _____ like just over a pound. That's perfect.
                          7

Lauren: What (do) _____ you _____ now with the
                          8   9
                soup?

David: It (smell) _____ great, so I (taste) _____ it.
                            10   11
                (want) _____ you _____ to taste it too?
                          12   13

Lauren: No, thanks. I (wait) _____ for everything to be
                                      14
                ready. I (prefer) _____ to taste it all at the same time.
                                      15

Activity 3   *(Review coordinating conjunctions: Unit One, pages 8–13.)*

A. *Find eight mistakes in the following conversation, and show how to correct each one.*

Jim: Hi, Susan. Thanks for helping me study today. I have trouble
                with the material we study in class this week.

Susan: Sure, no problem. I am needing to review some things, so this
                is good for me too. Where are you wanting to begin?

Jim: First of all, I am knowing there are nine learning styles in
                Gardner's theory, but . . . .

Susan: Wait a minute. I am thinking you are confusing the learning
                styles with Gardner's theory of multiple intelligences. There are
                three learning styles: visual, auditory, and tactile/kinesthetic,

but they are not the same as the nine kinds of intelligence in Gardner's theory.

Jim: What are you meaning? I am not understanding this now.

 B. In the following paragraph a professor is reviewing some material in a psychology class. Find six verb mistakes and correct each one.

Last week we learned about two different subjects: learning styles and the theory of multiple intelligences. They are seeming similar, for they describe some of the same characteristics. For example, a person who is having a tactile/kinesthetic learning style likes to learn through doing and manipulating things with hands-on experiences. This person might also be strong in Gardner's bodily/kinesthetic intelligence as well as a combination of other kinds of intelligence, such as naturalist and interpersonal. That is meaning this person may be a tactile/kinesthetic learner, yet she/he also has a unique combination of types of intelligence. A different tactile/kinesthetic learner might have another specific combination of kinds of intelligence. Do you all starting to understand the difference now? Are you seeing that the learning styles and the theory of intelligences are containing some overlap, but they are not exactly the same thing?

Activity 4

Choose two classes or outside activities that you are participating in this semester. Write three or four sentences about each, using one of the verbs listed below in each sentence. Do not use any verb more than one time.

EXAMPLE:

Name of class/activity: English Composition 120

1. I love my English class this semester, and I am improving my writing skills.

2. The book contains a lot of helpful information.

3. I feel good about my work in this class.

4. I notice some improvement in my essay writing, but I want to improve more.

VERBS:	like	dislike	forget	remember	cost
	understand	need	want	feel	have

Name of class/activity: _____

1. _____

2. _____

3. _____

4. _____

Name of class/activity: _____

1. _____

2. _____

3. _____

4. _____

Activity 5

Think about the nine different types of intelligence in Gardner's theory:

1. visual/spatial	2. verbal/linguistic	3. mathematical/logical
4. bodily/kinesthetic	5. musical/rhythmic	6. interpersonal
7. intrapersonal	8. naturalist	9. existentialist

Think about something in your life that relates to one of the nine kinds of intelligence. Write at least three sentences about things you sometimes do and something you are doing now that fit your strengths. Do not write the actual kind(s) of intelligence. Be sure to use some stative verbs and vocabulary words from this unit.

After you write these sentences, share them with a partner and ask this person to guess which kind(s) of intelligence you think you have.

EXAMPLE:

I love music and I know how to play several instruments. Right now I have a guitar and a banjo. I want to learn how to play the piano as well.

Your Partner: You probably have musical/rhythmic intelligence.

Future

Will/Be Going To

Presentation

Predictions: [1]Janelle **will be** a successful actress. [2]She **is going to perform** in many films and one day **will become** famous.

Plans: [3]Jamal **is making** plans for his future. [4]He **is going to work** as a doctor. [5]When **will** he **start** his first job?

Questions

1. What is the time of the caption for the first picture? How do you know this? What words give you information about the time?

2. What form of the verb follows the word *will* each time it appears? What form of the verb follows the expression *be going to* each time it appears?

Explanation—Future: Predictions and Plans

1. *Will* + verb (simple form)

    She *will (She'll*) become* an actress.
    He *will (He'll*) start* his first job soon.

---

*Contractions are often used in conversation. They are not usually used in formal writing.

2. *Be going to* **+ verb (simple form)**

   NOTE: Be sure to change the auxiliary *be* to agree with the subject.

   He *is (He's*) going to start* a new job next month. They *are (They're*) going to graduate* next month.

3. Use these forms for predictions.

   A prediction announces a future event before it happens.

   She/he *is (She/he's) going to perform* in many films. One day she/he *will (she'll/he'll) become* famous.

4. Use these forms for plans or intentions.

   He *is (He's) going to graduate* next month. Then he *will (he'll) start* a new job.

   USAGE NOTE: *Be going to* is used more often for plans than *will* is used for this meaning, especially in conversation.

5. Time words that indicate future time

   - next week/month/year/ Monday/March, etc.
   - in three hours/days/weeks
   - tonight/later/tomorrow
   - two days/weeks/months from now

   NOTE: You may not always see time words or expressions with *will* and *be going to* because we know the time is future from the meaning of these words.

6. **Negative sentences**

   RULE: Add the word *not* after the auxiliary to make a sentence negative.

   He *is not (isn't*) going to graduate* next month, and he *will not (won't*) start* a new job.

Follow this pattern for negative sentences using will and be going to:

subject	auxiliary	not	verb (simple form) or *going to* + verb	
He	will	not	start	a new job.
He	is	not	going to graduate	next month.
I	am	not	going to graduate	next month.

---

*Contractions are often used in conversation. They are not usually used in formal writing.

7. **Questions**

   a. **Yes/no questions**

   RULE: Place the auxiliary to the left of the subject of the sentence.

   Is he going to graduate next month. *Will he start* a new job?

Follow this pattern for yes/no questions using will and be going to:

auxiliary	subject	verb (simple form) or *going to* + verb	
Will	he	start	a new job?
Is	he	going to graduate	next month?
Are	they	going to graduate	next month?

   b. **Question word questions**

   RULE: Add the question word and place the auxiliary to the left of the subject to make the sentence a question.

   When is he *going to graduate? When will* he *start* the job?

Follow this pattern for question word questions using *will* and *be going to:*

question word	auxiliary	subject	verb (simple form) or *going to* + verb	
When	is	he	going to graduate?	
When	are	you	going to graduate?	
When	will	he	start	the job?
Who	will		graduate	next month?
Who	is		going to graduate	this year?
What	is		going to start	next week?
What	will		start	next week?

Practice

Activity 1

A. *Fill in the blank spaces in the following predictions using the words given in parentheses. Then indicate which intelligence(s) of the nine in Gardner's theory are probably these people's strengths.*

1. Tom (will/get) _____ a job as a salesperson in an electronics store.

   intelligence (s): _____

2. Scot (be going to/find) _____ a job at an environmental agency.

   intelligence(s): _____

3. Lisa and Steve (be going to /become) _____ school counselors.

   intelligence(s): _____

4. Alicia (will/enroll) _____ in a school that specializes in music and art.

   intelligence(s): _____

B. *Write three or four predictions about your future job or career, using* will *for some predictions and* be going to *for others. What kind(s) of intelligence do these relate to?*

Activity 2

A. *Read the following sentences about people's plans to improve their abilities in their weak areas. Find five mistakes and show how to correct them.*

1. José be going to try to improve his bodily/kinesthetic intelligence. He will joins a gym and he will try to build his physical strength.

2. Barbara is going take guitar lessons. She wills study the piano also because she wants to improve her musical ability.

3. Janet and Allen is going to become more outgoing because they know they are somewhat quiet and shy people. They will try to think of strategies to make new friends.

B. *Which kind(s) of intelligence would you like to improve? Write three or four plans to improve your own areas of intelligence, using* will *for some plans and* be going to *for others.*

Activity 3

Interview a partner about his/her plans and predictions for the future. First, write questions using the information given and either will *or* be going to *in each question. Then, interview your partner by asking these questions. After you ask each question, write your partner's answer.*

Plans

1. _____

   what / do / at the end of this course

   Answer: _____

2. _____

   how many more classes / take / this year

   Answer: _____

3. _____

   how much longer / study / at this school

   Answer: _____

Predictions

1. _____

   where / live / in five years

   Answer: _____

2. _____

   what kind of job / have / in 10 years

   Answer: _____

3. _____

   which kind of intelligence / you / improve / in the future

   Answer: _____

Explanation 2—More about *Will* and *Be Going To*

Will and *be going to* are not used only to express future predictions and plans. The chart below shows the various meanings and uses for these two ways of discussing the future.

	will	be going to
predictions	You **will become** a successful filmmaker.	You **are going to become** a successful filmmaker.
plans*	He **will take** that algebra class next semester for his math requirements.	He **is going to take** that algebra class next semester for his math requirements.
promises	• Did you give me your revised paper? • No, but I **will bring** it to your office before 3 p.m.	
offers to help	• The phone is ringing. • I**'ll get** it.	
a decision to do something made at the moment of speaking	A: Did you hear about Dr. Orr's lecture in the Student Center this evening at 7 p.m.? B: I love to hear her speak. I think I**'ll go**.	
An expectation about the very near future based on something the speaker sees/knows at the moment of speaking		Watch that pitcher of water near the edge of the table. It**'s going to fall**.

*Note: Native speakers use *be going to* + verb more often than *will* for plans, especially in conversation.

Activity 4

Label the use of will *or* be going to *in each sentence as a promise* (P), *a decision* (D), *an offer to help* (O), *or an expectation* (E).

1. Teacher: You need to add this class before the deadline.

_____   Student: Okay. I'll do it before next Monday.

_____ 2. Student: The graded tests are on the instructor's desk. He's going to return them to us today.

3. Student 1: Are you going to the special study session after class?

_____   Student 2: I didn't know about it. I need the extra help, so I'll go.

4. Student: There's too much light in the room. I can't see the information on the screen.

_____   Teacher: I'll turn out that light to help make it more clear.

_____ 5. Student: I just saw my grades for this class. I think I'll go to the tutoring session for help on this new paper I'm writing.

_____ 6. Teacher: I'm not sure how many units you need to finish your major. I'll get that information for you by tomorrow.

7. Student 1: I think I added too much of this chemical in the bottle for this experiment.

_____   Student 2: Watch out! It's going to spill over and get all over your hands and the table.

8. Teacher: I forgot to bring my bag with me, so I may not be able to carry all these portfolios to my office.

_____   Student: I'll carry some of them for you. I'm walking in the direction of your office anyway.

Activity 5   (*Review coordinating conjunctions: Unit One, pages 8–13.*)

Read the situations below and write a sentence for each one. Be sure to use will *or* be going to *in each of your answers.*

1. You advisor is explaining two different English classes to you. One class is five hours per week and includes both reading and writing. The other class is three hours a week and is only about reading. Tell your advisor your decision about which class to sign up for.

    _____

    _____

2. Your friend was absent last class, so he doesn't understand the homework assignment. Make an offer to work with your friend and help him complete the assignment.

    _____

    _____

3. You are working on a presentation with a partner in your class. She can't finish her part of the work, for you didn't add the information you found in the library. Make a promise to give her that information later today.

    _____

    _____

4. Your friend is searching through her backpack for a book she needs. She also has some books on her desk. She is accidentally pushing them to the edge of the desk, and they are almost ready to fall off. Tell your friend what you expect to happen to her books.

    _____

    _____

5. Your friend says she cannot understand the instructor's lectures very well, so she would like to tape them. However, she does not have enough money to buy her own tape recorder. Make an offer to let her borrow yours.

_____

_____

6. You are playing soccer on an outdoor field for one of your PE classes, and all of a sudden the clouds are getting very dark. Tell your classmates what you expect to happen soon.

_____

_____

7. It's the end of the semester, and your friend is asking you about your summer plans. Tell him what you plan to do for the summer.

_____

_____

8. You and a friend are discussing some ideas about your futures. Make a prediction to your friend about your situation two years from now.

_____

_____

Future

Present Progressive (Continuous*) and Simple Present

[1]Tomorrow Seth **is starting** his first job as a college graduate. [2]He **is taking** a 6 a.m. train to be sure he **arrives** at the office early. [3]His office **opens** at 7 a.m. tomorrow, and he wants to get there right on time.

Presentation

Questions

1. Circle the verbs in bold in this caption. Put a line under any time words you see. What is the time in these sentences?

2. Is there anything unusual about the verb forms in this caption and the time of the sentences? What did you learn in the previous lessons about these verb forms? How are they used differently in this caption?

Explanation—Using Present Progressive (Continuous*) and Simple Present Forms

1. Native speakers often use the present progressive form to talk about plans. This form is most often used in conversation or informal writing.

   Tomorrow Seth *is starting* his first job as a college graduate. He *is taking* a 6 a.m. train to work.

2. The simple present form of some verbs may also indicate future events. These verbs often indicate information about scheduled activities and events. Following is a list of verbs commonly used this way:

arrive	depart	leave	come	go
begin	start	end	finish	
return	open	close	graduate	

   The train *arrives* at 5:00 p.m. tonight. They *graduate* next May. The movie *begins* in an hour.

---

*Note: Sometimes the word *continuous* is used in place of the word *progressive*. These words have the same meaning.

3. When you use these forms to indicate future time, be sure to use a future time word or expression in your sentence or story. If you do not use these words, the time may be confusing.

> The train *arrives* on track 5. Is this every day or later today or tomorrow?

> The guest lecturer *is speaking* in Room 220. Is this right now or later or another day in the future?

> Without more information we cannot be sure about the time in these examples.

Practice

Activity 1

State whether the time in each of the following sentences is general time (G), present time (P), or future time (F). Be prepared to explain your answers.

_____ 1. Today I am starting my first semester at a new school.

_____ 2. I usually get very nervous on the first day of new classes.

_____ 3. However, today for some reason I feel calm and ready to go.

_____ 4. I am going to attend my first class for my major tomorrow.

_____ 5. I will work very hard in that class to make sure I get a good grade.

_____ 6. I always worry about doing well in school and getting good grades.

_____ 7. Right now I am trying to make sure I have all my books and supplies.

_____ 8. This evening I will start any homework assignments from today's classes.

Activity 2   *(Review coordinating conjunctions: Unit One, pages 8–13.)*

Find and correct two mistakes in each of the following paragraphs.

1. Nancy wants to improve her visual/spatial intelligence. She going to take a drawing class next week. Another class about painting starts in two weeks. She is trying to figure out a way to take both classes, but it is not going be possible because they are both on the same nights.

2. Dan is attending a field seminar class this semester, and the class making its first trip next weekend. The bus leaves at 6 a.m. on Saturday, and the professor expects everyone to be on time. Dan is get up at 5 a.m. to make sure he won't miss the bus.

3. Ed's classes begins on Friday. He is taking night classes this semester because he works every day until 5 p.m. Parking is always bad for the first few days of classes, so he is leaves work early to find a parking spot.

Activity 3

It is the start of a new semester, and two students are talking about their classes and schedules for this term. Circle the correct form(s) of the verb in parentheses. In some cases more than one answer may be correct. Underline time words and expressions as well.

Jim: Hey, Helen! How are your classes this semester? (Are you going/Do you go) to one this afternoon?

Helen: Yes, in fact I (am going to start/am starting) two new classes today, one at 3 p.m. and one tonight at 7 p.m. What about you? How are your classes?

Jim: I (am having/had) my first class this morning, and it was great. Now I (wait/am waiting) for my next class. It (begins/begin/going to begin) in about half an hour.

Helen: Which class is that? (Are you taking/Do you take) any math classes this semester?

Jim: No, I finished my math requirements. It's a geography class. This semester I (am working on/will work on/work on) classes for my major. In fact, I am almost finished with all of my classes for my degree. I (graduate/am graduating) at the end of next semester.

Helen: That's great. I (need/am needing) several more classes for my major, so I (stay/am staying/am going to stay) at this school for at least one more year.

Jim: Well, it's time for me to get to my next class. I (am not wanting/don't want) to be late for the first one. Good luck this semester.

Helen: Thanks. You too.

Activity 4

A. Carol needs to see one of her professors to get some help with the material they are studying in class, but her schedule does not fit the professor's office hours. Right now they are discussing their schedules to find a good time to meet next week. Look at their schedules below and write some questions and answers they might be saying. One has been done for you as an example. You may continue that conversation.

	Carol's schedule						Dr. Johns' schedule				
	Mon.	Tues.	Wed.	Thurs.	Fri.		Mon.	Tues.	Wed.	Thurs.	Fri.
8						8					
9	class		class			9	office		office		lab
10	class		class		work	10	office	class	office	class	lab
11	class		class		work	11	class	class	class	class	
12					work	12	class	class	class	class	
1	work	class	work	class		1		office		office	
2	work	class	work	class		2		office		office	
3	work		work			3					
4						4					

Carol: Thanks for making a special appointment for me next week. Are you available on Tuesday at 11 a.m.?

Dr. Johns: No, sorry. I'm teaching at that time. The class ends at 12:45. Can you meet then?

B. *Write your own schedule for this week. Then work with a partner to make a study date for next week with him/her. Do not show each other your schedules. Try to agree on a date and time to study together.*

My schedule				
Mon.	Tues.	Wed.	Thurs.	Fri.
8				
9				
10				
11				
12				
1				
2				
3				
4				

Past Progressive (Continuous*)

¹In 1838 Frederick Bailey **was working** in a Baltimore shipyard, but he was still a slave. ²At that same time he and some free black friends **were making** plans for his escape to freedom. ³He made this escape when he took a train to Philadelphia on September 3, 1838.

Presentation 1

Questions

1. What ending is on the verbs in bold in sentences 1 and 2? What helping verbs (auxiliaries) do you see just before these verbs?

2. Circle the verbs in sentence 3. Why don't these verbs have the same endings as the verbs in bold in sentences 1 and 2?

Explanation—Past Progressive (Continuous*)

1. **Past of auxiliary** *be (was/were)* + **verb** + *-ing*

    Be sure to have all three of these pieces, including the *-ing* ending. This ending tells you the action was in progress or lasted a long time.

    In 1838 Frederick Bailey *was working* in a shipyard.
                                        1   2   3

    At the same time he *was making* plans to escape to freedom.
                               1   2   3

2. **Verbs with spelling changes** (See Appendix G for rules.)

    In 1838 Frederick *was living* in Baltimore.

    In 1838 Frederick and his friends *were planning* his escape.

---

*Note: Sometimes the word *continuous* is used in place of the word *progressive*. These words have the same meaning.

3. Use these verb forms for past actions that were in progress or continuous at a certain time in the past. The actions started before that specific time, were in progress at that time, and perhaps continued beyond that time.

> In 1838 Frederick Bailey *was working* in a shipyard. At the same time he *was planning* his escape.

Do not use these forms for one-time completed actions in the past.

> On September 3, 1838 he *took* a train to freedom.

Do not use these forms for stative (non-action) verbs. (See Lesson 4 page 24.)

> Frederick and his friends *understood* the dangers of trying to escape. They *realized* it was dangerous but possible.

4. **Negative sentences**

RULE: Add the word *not* after the auxiliary to make a sentence negative.

> Frederick *was not (wasn't*)* working in a Baltimore shipyard.
> His friends *were not (weren't*)* planning his escape with him.

Follow this pattern for negative sentences using past progressive verb forms:

subject	auxiliary *(be)*	not	verb + *-ing*	
Frederick	was	not	working	in a Baltimore shipyard.
His friends	were	not	planning	his escape with him.

5. **Questions**

   a. **Yes/no questions**

RULE: Place the auxiliary to the left of the subject.

> *Was* Frederick *working* in a Baltimore shipyard? *Were* his friends *planning* his escape with him?

Follow this pattern for yes/no questions with past progressive verb forms:

auxiliary *(be)*	subject	verb + *-ing*	
Was	Frederick	working	in a Baltimore shipyard?
Were	his friends	planning	his escape with him?

   b. **Question word questions**

RULE: Add the question word and place the auxiliary to the left of the subject.

> *When was* Fredrick *working* in a shipyard? *Why were* his friends *planning* his escape with him?

---

*Contractions are often used in conversation. They are not usually used in formal writing.

Follow this pattern for question word questions with past progressive verbs:

question word	auxiliary *(be)*	subject	verb + *-ing*	
When	was	Frederick	working	in a shipyard?
Why	were	his friends	planning	his escape with him?
Who	was		trying	to escape with friends?
What	was		making	the escape difficult?

Practice

Activity 1

Complete the following sentences with the past progressive of one of the verbs below. Use each verb only one time.

struggle	live	meet	learn	work

1. Before 1824 Frederick Bailey _____ with his grandmother in a cabin.

2. In 1826 many slaves _____ in the fields on the plantation with him.

3. In 1827 Frederick _____ how to read at the Auld's house in Baltimore.

4. In 1834 he _____ to survive on Thomas Covey's farm.

5. In 1836 Frederick and other slaves _____ to plan an escape.

Activity 2   *(Review coordinating conjunctions: Unit One, pages 8–13.)*

Find eight mistakes in the following paragraph about Frederick Douglass. Show how to correct each mistake.

In 1826 Frederick Douglass move to Baltimore to live with Hugh and Sophia Auld. At first Sophia was teach him to read, for she was a kind woman. Then her husband became furious when he was learning about this, and he told her to stop. Frederick was wanting to learn more, so he were learning on his own. During that time he was runing many errands for the Aulds, so he could meet people on the streets of the city. Poor white children was teaching him more and more about reading. By the time he was 13, he reading enough to learn about abolitionists.

Activity 3   *(Review coordinating conjunctions: Unit One, pages 8–13.)*

Fill in the blank spaces below using either the simple past or the past progressive form of the verbs in parentheses. In some cases either one may be correct, but you should use the past progressive form wherever possible.

A.   Plantation slaves (have) _____ a difficult life. By 6:00 or 7:00 in
      the morning they (work) _____ in the fields. All day long they
      (do) _____ difficult work, and they (get—negative)
      _____ time for breaks.

B.   On Frederick's plantation, the owner (give—negative) _____
      the slaves much food, so Frederick and the other slave children (starve)
      _____ much of the time.

C.   Thomas Covey (used to beat) _____ his slaves, and Frederick
      often (receive) _____ these beatings. One day Covey (tie)
      _____ Frederick to a post in order to give him a whipping, but
      Frederick stopped him by fighting back.

D.   At age 17 Frederick (start) _____ an illegal school for Blacks.
      For many months he (teach) _____ other slaves to read, and he
      (help) _____ plan their escape to freedom.

E.   Frederick (feel) _____ nervous during his escape north, for he
      (know) _____ he could get caught. He was successful partly
      because on the train he (carry) _____ papers from a free black
      sailor.

Presentation 2—Past Progressive (Continuous) with Time Clauses

When Frederick **moved** to Baltimore, he **was living** with the Aulds and **taking care of** their baby. While he **was running** errands for the Aulds, he **met** some poor white children in the street. Later, as he **was running** the errands, he **was** also **paying** these children to teach him to read.

Questions

1. Do all of the verbs in bold in these sentences have the same endings? How and why are they different?

2. What is the time of the verbs in bold? Which of these actions happened or finished quickly and which ones did not?

Explanation—Past Progressive (Continuous) with Time Clauses

You will often find past progressive forms with time clauses that begin with the conjunctions *when, while,* and *as.* (Refer to Unit Two, pages 42–49 of *Destinations 2: Writing for Academic Success* for a review of sentences with these words.)

1. Sometimes one clause uses the simple past, and the other clause uses past progressive. In these sentences, one action is short or finished, but the other action is in progress (not finished) or longer.

   > When Frederick *moved* to Baltimore, he *was living* with the Aulds and *taking care of* their baby.

2. In some cases, the action in one clause comes in the middle of or interrupts the action in the other clause.

   > While he *was running* errands for the Aulds, he *met* some poor white
   > <small>not finished</small>   <small>interruption</small>
   > children in the street.

   > While Sophie Auld *was teaching* Frederick to read, her husband
   > *became* angry.   <small>not finished</small>
   > <small>interruption</small>

3. In other cases, both clauses use the past progressive because both actions were continuous.

   > As he *was running* these errands, he *was paying* these children to teach him to read.

   > As Sophie's husband *was telling* her not to teach Frederick to read, Frederick *was paying* attention to their conversation.

Practice

Activity 4   *(Review subordinating conjunctions: Unit Two, pages 42–49.)*

Read the following statements about Frederick Douglass and another slave, Harriet Tubman, and then answer the questions that follow as True (T) or False (F).

1. Frederick Douglass and Harriet Tubman were both born around the same time, and in the 1820s both of them were growing up on plantations in Maryland.

   _____ In the 1820s both Frederick Douglass and Harriet Tubman were adults.

2. When Frederick was living with his grandmother as a young child, Harriet was also spending her childhood with her grandmother.

   _____ Frederick Douglass and Harriet Tubman were living with their grandmothers at the same time.

3. When Frederick escaped to freedom in 1838, Harriet was still working as a slave.

   _____ Frederick became free before Harriet escaped to freedom.

4. While Frederick was writing his second book in 1851, Harriet Tubman was bringing slaves to freedom on the Underground Railroad.

   _____ Frederick Douglass finished his second book before Harriet Tubman worked on the Underground Railroad.

Activity 5   *(Review subordinating conjunctions: Unit Two, pages 42–49.)*

Fill in the spaces with the simple past or past progressive form of the verb in parentheses. Use the past progressive wherever possible.

A. When Harriet Tubman (live) _____ with her grandmother for

   the first few years of her life, she (work—negative) _____ as

   a slave.

B. When Harriet Tubman (be) _____ six years old, she (work)

   _____ as a house servant for a family. While she (stay)

   _____ with this family, she (become) _____ sick with

   the measles, so she (go) _____ back to her master.

C. When Harriet was about 16 years old, she (have) _____ a bad
8
accident when she (try) _____ to help another slave. As her
9
master (throw) _____ a rock at the other slave, Harriet (run)
10
_____ to protect the man, and the rock (hit) _____
11   12
her in the head.

D. In 1849 Harriet (escape) _____ to freedom. As she (escape)
13
_____ , she (use) _____ the North Star to guide her in
14   15
the right direction.

E. By 1850 she (make) _____ many trips south as a conductor on
16
the Underground Railroad to bring other slaves to freedom. While she

(take) _____ slaves up north, she (enforce) _____
17   18
rules for the escape, and she never (lose) _____ anyone on any
19
of her trips.

Activity 6

A. *Look at the following timeline and think about your life during any of these years. Write an X three or four times on this line. Above each X write where you were or what you were doing at that time. (You should write only a word or two for each one.) You will find one example on the time line.*

in college
X
+———+———+———+———+———+———+———+———+———+———+———+
1950 1955 1960 1965 1970 1975 1980 1985 1990 1995 2000 2005

B. *Now write two or three sentences about what you did or were doing at each time. Use a simple past form and a past progressive form of the verb in each sentence.*

EXAMPLES:

In 2001 I was a student.   I was studying in college.

_____

_____

_____

_____

_____

_____

C. *Work in groups of three and discuss your answers. Together, write as many sentences as you can discussing what each of you were doing at the same time on the timeline. Use* when, while, *or* as *in your sentences as much as possible.*

EXAMPLE:

When I was taking classes in college, Claudia was working at a bank.

_____

_____

_____

_____

_____

_____

_____

Present Perfect

Indefinite Past/Repeated Past

[1]The Constitution of the United States contains the laws that govern this country, and it allows for changes or amendments. [2]As a result, Congress **has submitted** amendments more than 30 times to the states for a vote. [3]The states **have ratified** these changes 26 times. [4]The last one **took** place in 1971.

Presentation

Questions

1. What is the time in sentence 4? How do you know this?

2. What ending is on the verbs in bold in sentences 2 and 3? What helping verbs (auxiliaries) do you see with these verbs?

3. Is the time in sentences 2 and 3 the same as the time in sentence 4? How do you know?

Explanation: Present Perfect—Indefinite Time/ Repeated Actions

1. Regular verbs: *have/has* + verb (past participle)

   past participle of regular verbs: verb + *-ed*

   Each state *has voted* on Constitutional amendments. Many states *have passed* these amendments. The states *have ratified* these changes. (Note *y* to *i* spelling change. See Appendix G for rule.)

2. **Past participle of irregular verbs: various endings** (See Appendix A for list of verbs.)

   We *have made* changes to the Constitution. These changes *have become* amendments.

3. **Negative sentences**

   RULE: Add the word *not* after the auxiliary to make a sentence negative.

   That state *has not (hasn't*) voted* to pass the amendment. Some amendments *have not (haven't*)passed.*

Follow this pattern for negative sentences with present perfect verb forms:

subject	auxiliary	*not*	verb (past participle)	
That state	has	not	voted	to pass the amendment.
Some amendments	have	not	passed.	

4. **Questions**

   a. **Yes/no questions**

   RULE: Place the auxiliary to the left of the subject of the sentence.

   Have some laws *changed? Has* that state *voted* to change the law?

Follow this pattern for yes/no questions with present perfect verb forms:

auxiliary	subject	verb (past participle)	
Have	some laws	changed?	
Has	that state	voted	to change the law?

   b. **Question word questions**

   Add the question word and place the auxiliary *have/has* to the left of the subject to make the sentence a question.

   Why have some laws *changed? How has* the Constitution *changed? Who has changed* the Constitution? *What has changed* in the Constitution?

Follow this pattern for question word questions with present perfect verb forms:

question word	auxiliary	subject	verb (past participle)	
Why	have	some laws	changed?	
How	has	the Constitution	changed?	
Who	has		changed	the Constitution?
What	has		changed	in the Constitution?

---

*Contractions are often used in conversation. They are not usually used in formal writing.

5. a.   Use the present perfect verb form for events in the past that took place (and finished) at an unspecified time or for repeated events. In these cases the time is not known or not important.

We *have made* amendments to the U.S. Constitution. (no specific time)
We *have changed* it 26 times. (repeated past)

   b.   Sometimes we use a present perfect form of the verb to introduce something that took place in general terms. Then we follow this with more specific information or details in the past simple tense. There is no time word with the present perfect form, but there could be a time word with the more specific information.

We *have attempted* to make amendments to the U.S. Constitution many times. The states *ratified* the last amendment in 1971.

6. We also use present perfect forms for people's accomplishments without specific time words.

That Senator *has worked* to change the law.

Remember: Do not use the present perfect with a specific time word.

In 1999 she *voted* to change the law. *Not:* In 1999 she ~~has voted~~ to change the law.

7. When we use present perfect forms, there is also a relationship or connection with the present. The action or event happened and finished in the past, but it often continues to affect/influence the present in some way. Therefore, we use these forms for accomplishments of living people.

Oprah Winfrey *has made* several movies. (connection with the present: She might make more.)

However, we do not use these forms to discuss accomplishments of people who are no longer living. We discuss these accomplishments with simple past verb forms.

Martin Luther King **won** a Nobel Peace Prize. He **was** a great orator.
NOT: Martin Luther King ~~has won~~ a Nobel Peace prize. He ~~has been~~ a great orator.

Practice

Activity 1

Fill in the spaces with the present perfect form of the verb in parentheses.

A. Lawmakers (introduce) _____ over 5,000 amendments in
    <u>1</u>
    Congress. However, only 26 of them (pass) _____ and
    <u>2</u>
    (become) _____ law.
    <u>3</u>

B. The president's oath of office (change—negative) _____. Each
    <u>4</u>
    of the presidents of the United States (take) _____ the same
    <u>5</u>
    oath of office as it appears in the Constitution.

C. Three presidents (Andrew Johnson, Richard Nixon, William Jefferson
    Clinton) of the United States (face) _____ impeachment. In
    <u>6</u>
    two cases (Johnson and Clinton), the House of Representatives voted to
    impeach them, but the Senate did not convict them. In the third case
    (Nixon), the President resigned before any vote could take place. Thus,
    Congress (remove—negative) _____ any president from office.
    <u>7</u>

Activity 2

*Fill in the spaces with either the present perfect or simple past form of the verb in
parentheses. Wherever possible, try to use the present perfect forms.*

A. Several amendments (give) _____ specific groups of people the
    <u>1</u>
    right to vote. The 15th Amendment, saying nobody can take the right
    to vote away from any citizen because of "race, color, or previous
    condition of servitude," (become) _____ law in 1879. The 19th
    <u>2</u>
    Amendment (grant) _____ the right to vote to women in
    <u>3</u>
    1920, and in 1971 the 26th Amendment (make) _____ the
    <u>4</u>
    legal voting age 18 instead of the previous age of 21.

B. The number of times one person can serve as president of the United
    States (change) _____. In 1951, the 22nd Amendment (go)
    <u>1</u>
    _____ into effect. This amendment (limit) _____ the
    <u>2</u>   <u>3</u>
    number of terms a U.S. president can serve to two.

C. The Constitution (have) _____ amendments about the
$_1$
sale of liquor twice. The prohibition of the sale of alcohol (begin)

_____ in 1920 with the passing of the 18th Amendment in
$_2$
1919. Then in 1933 the states (repeal) _____ that law with the
$_3$
21st Amendment.

 ### Activity 3

Find a total of six mistakes in the following information about accomplishments in different people's lives and correct them.

1. Frederick Douglass IV, the great-great-grandson of the famous
    abolitionist, have created an organization called the Frederick Douglass
    Organization Inc. He started this organization to give lectures and re-
    create the speeches and messages of his famous ancestor.

2. Two African-Americans, Thurgood Marshall and Clarence Thomas, has
    served as Supreme Court Justices. Thurgood Marshall (the grandson of a
    slave) has become the first one in 1987.

3. African-Americans have made great achievements in sports. Some of
    them has competed at the Olympics. For example, in 1936 Jesse Owens
    won four gold medals in track and field, and in 1960 Muhammad Ali
    won the gold medal in boxing at age 18.

4. Many African-Americans have serve in the Congress of the United States
    as representatives of their states. Shirley Chisholm was the first African-
    American woman to do so in 1968.

5. A few African-Americans have ran for the presidency of the United
    States. For example, Shirley Chisholm ran in 1972, and Jesse Jackson ran
    in 1984.

Activity 4

A. Write two sentences about changes you have made in your life. (Think about any part of your life, such as school, family, job, etc.) Use present perfect verb forms and do not use any time words in your sentences.

1. _____

2. _____

B. Discuss your answers with your classmates. Write some of their answers below. Ask your classmates follow-up questions to learn more.

1. My classmate (_____) _____
                     (name)
   _____

2. My classmate (_____) _____
                     (name)

   _____

C. What accomplishments have you made in your life? Write sentences about one or two of your accomplishments using the present perfect form of the verb for each accomplishment. Then write another sentence with a detail about this accomplishment using a time word or expression and the simple past.

EXAMPLE: I have graduated from high school. In 2001 I received my high school diploma.

   Share your statements with the rest of the class. Try to complete as many of the sentences below as possible. Be sure to use present perfect verb forms in your answers.

1. My classmates (_____ and _____) _____
                      (name)   (name)
   _____

2. My classmates (_____ and _____) _____
                      (name)   (name)

   _____

3. We (my classmate _____ and I) _____
                          (name)
   _____

4. We (my classmate _____ and I) _____
                          (name)
   _____

Activity 5

Think of a famous living person. Write two or three sentences about this person's accomplishments using present perfect forms of the verbs. Then write two or three more sentences including specific information (with dates if you can). Do not write the name of this person in your sentences. Read your sentences to a partner or the class, and have them guess who the person is.

1. _____

2. _____

3. _____

4. _____

5. _____

6. _____

Present Perfect with Adverbs

(never/recently/just/already/finally/ ever/yet/until now/up to now/so far)

[1]Some students from my school **have recently returned** from a visit to Washington, D.C. [2]One of them **has just finished** giving an oral presentation to the class about the trip. [3]She started the presentation by asking, "**Have** you **ever been** to Washington, D.C.?"

Presentation

Questions

1. What form of the verbs do you see in bold in sentences 1 and 2?

2. Where do you see the words *recently* and *just* in relation to these verbs? How is the word *ever* different in sentence 3? What kind of sentence do you find it in?

3. What can you say about the time in sentences 1 and 2? Is the writer talking about only one time, or is the writer making a relationship between two times? When did these things happen in relation to the time the writer is discussing them?

Explanation—Present Perfect with Adverbs

1. Present perfect with adverbs: *have/has* + adverb + verb (past participle)

   Some adverbs often appear between the auxiliary *(have/has)* and the verb (past participle).

   These are some adverbs of time: *never, recently, just, already, finally*

   > Some students *have recently returned* home from a trip.
   >
   > One student *has just finished* giving on oral presentation to the class.

   Some of these words *(recently/finally/already)* may also appear at the beginning or end of a sentence.

   > Some students *have recently returned* home. *Recently* some students *have returned* home. Some students *have returned* home *recently*.

2. All of these words help to make a relationship or connection between something that took place in the past and the present. These words may indicate an effect or result of the past event on a current situation. Each word has a different meaning as follows:

never: at no time in the past (and maybe including now)

   I *have never visited* Washington D.C.

recently: in the near past; not very long ago

   Some students *have recently returned* home.

just: very close to now; very recently

   Some students *have just returned* from their trip to Washington, D.C.

already: at some time in the past

   I *have already read* that book. (Perhaps now I want to read another book, or perhaps I am now prepared for a test about that book.)

finally: at long last

   I *have finally finished* reading that difficult assignment. (It took a long time.)

3. *Up to now/until now/so far*

These expressions indicate any time from the past until now. They usually appear at the beginning or end of a sentence.

   (So far) we *have studied* one unit about the history of the United States *(so far).*

   (Until now /Up to now) we *have read* one story about Harriet Tubman *(until now).*

4. **Negative sentences**

RULE: Add the word *not* after the auxiliary to make a sentence negative. (See Lesson 8 in this book for a review.)

   I *have not (haven't) recently visited* Washington, D.C. *So far* we *have not (haven't) learned* about the Civil War.

Do *not* make negative sentences with these verb forms and *never.* This will make two negatives in the sentence, and this is not acceptable.

   INCORRECT: ~~I haven't never visited Washington, D.C.~~

5. **Questions**

RULE: Move the auxiliary to the left of the subject. (See Lesson 8 in this book for a review.)

Review these same samples for adverb placement.

   Has she *(recently) visited* the Lincoln Memorial *(recently)?*
   (So far) have you *taken* any tests in that class *(so far)?*
   How many tests have you *(already) taken* in that class *(already)?*

Do not make questions with present perfect verb forms and *never*.

INCORRECT: Have you never been to Paris?

CORRECT: Have you ever been to Paris?

6. *Ever* and *yet*

These words do not work the same way as the other words because they are used in negative sentences and questions only. In addition, *yet* is placed at the end of the sentence or question.

Have you ever read that book? (at any time) *Have you read* those books *yet*? (until now)

No, I *haven't ever read* that book. (OR, No, I *have never read* that book.)

No, I *haven't read* that book *yet*.

Practice

Activity 1   *(Review coordinating conjunctions: Unit One, pages 8–13.)*

Fill in the blanks using the present perfect form of the verb and the word or expression given in parentheses. Then answer the questions that follow as true (T) or false (F).

In my history class we (complete—recently) _____ the first

chapter, and the teacher (assign—just) _____ a new reading for

the second chapter. We (read—already) _____ about slavery

and the abolitionists, but we (finish—yet) _____ all of the

discussions about that _____ . _____ in this class we

(have—so far) _____ only one short quiz, but the teacher

(give—never) _____ us a long test. Yesterday she told us we will

have an essay exam next week. Some of us (write—ever) _____

an essay in class, so we are a little nervous about that.

_____ 1. This class finished the first chapter of the book a long time ago.

_____ 2. The teacher probably assigned the new reading within the last one or two days.

_____ 3. The class had some discussions about the U.S. Civil War, and they will not have any more.

_____ 4. The teacher has never given any quizzes or tests in this class.

_____ 5. Some students are nervous because they will have to write an in-class essay next week.

Activity 2   *(Review coordinating conjunctions: Unit One, pages 8–13 and subordinating*
conjunctions: Unit Two, pages 42–49.)

Read the e-mail messages below. Find and correct twelve mistakes.

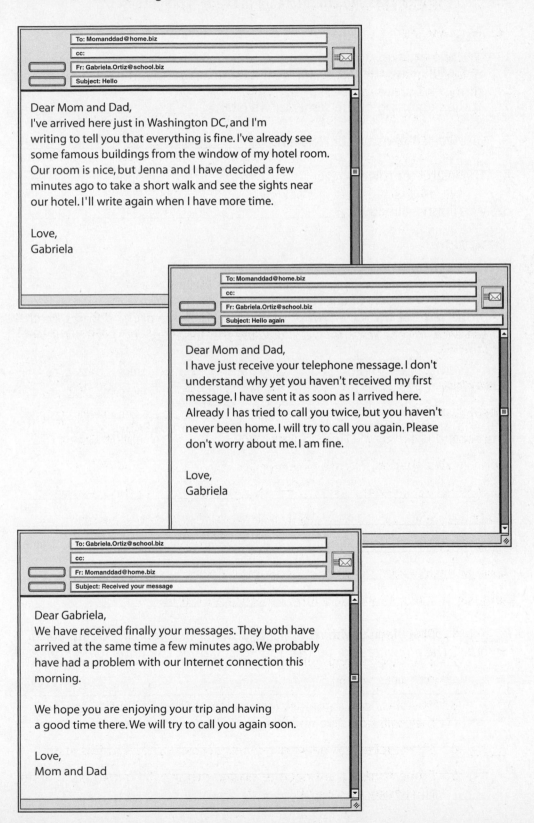

To: Momanddad@home.biz

cc:

Fr: Gabriela.Ortiz@school.biz

Subject: Hello

Dear Mom and Dad,
I've arrived here just in Washington DC, and I'm
writing to tell you that everything is fine. I've already see
some famous buildings from the window of my hotel room.
Our room is nice, but Jenna and I have decided a few
minutes ago to take a short walk and see the sights near
our hotel. I'll write again when I have more time.

Love,
Gabriela

To: Momanddad@home.biz

cc:

Fr: Gabriela.Ortiz@school.biz

Subject: Hello again

Dear Mom and Dad,
I have just receive your telephone message. I don't
understand why yet you haven't received my first
message. I have sent it as soon as I arrived here.
Already I has tried to call you twice, but you haven't
never been home. I will try to call you again. Please
don't worry about me. I am fine.

Love,
Gabriela

To: Gabriela.Ortiz@school.biz

cc:

Fr: Momanddad@home.biz

Subject: Received your message

Dear Gabriela,
We have received finally your messages. They both have
arrived at the same time a few minutes ago. We probably
have had a problem with our Internet connection this
morning.

We hope you are enjoying your trip and having
a good time there. We will try to call you again soon.

Love,
Mom and Dad

Activity 3

Complete the following sentences about one of your classes this semester using the simple past or present perfect form of the verb in parentheses.

Class: _____

1. So far this semester we (complete) _____

2. At the beginning of the semester we (start) _____

3. Last week the instructor (explain) _____

4. The instructor (give—yet) _____

5. We (finish—already) _____

Activity 4

A. *Write five sentences about your activities/experiences in the last year. Use one of the verbs below (or a verb of your choice) and one of the adverbs in each sentence. In each sentence you should use the present perfect form of the verb.*

> verbs: see   read   study   visit   enjoy   finish   take   pass
>   have   be

> adverbs: already   recently   finally   up to/until now   so far
>   just   never

1. _____

2. _____

3. _____

4. _____

5. _____

B. *Share your sentences with a partner by reading your sentences aloud to each other. Then, rewrite your partner's sentences, using* she *or* he *for the subject.*

1. _____

2. _____

3. _____

4. _____

5. _____

Activity 5

A. *Read the following questions and answer them truthfully.*

If the answer to a question is no, write a sentence using the present perfect form of the verb and *never* or *ever.* If the answer is yes, write two sentences as follows:

1. Write a sentence using the present perfect form of the verb.
2. Write another sentence that gives a specific detail using the simple past.

EXAMPLE:

Have you ever climbed to the top of Mt. Everest?

No, I have never climbed to the top of Mt. Everest. OR

No, I haven't ever climbed to the top of Mt. Everest.

Yes, I have climbed Mt. Everest. I climbed to the top in 1992.

1. Have you ever visited any historical places near your town or city?

    _____

    _____

2. Have you ever read a book at least 100 pages long in English?

    _____

    _____

3. Have you ever worked with the soil on a farm?

    _____

    _____

4. Have you ever done something dangerous?

    _____

    _____

5. Have you ever lived in a cabin?

    _____

    _____

6. Have you ever swum in the Indian Ocean?

    _____

    _____

7. Have you ever ridden in a helicopter?

_____

_____

8. Have you ever seen a UFO?

_____

_____

B. *Now write a few* Have you ever . . . *questions of your own. Try to think of unusual things to ask your classmates. Then read your questions to the class and see if anyone has ever done those things.*

You may want to play this as a game with your class. You will receive one point if the answer to your question is "No!" Remember to keep your questions unusual *but* realistic.

1. _____

2. _____

3. _____

4. _____

Present Perfect

From Past to Present with For and Since

1955 ——————————— now

[1]Many Jim Crow laws **have changed since 1955.** [2]Laws such as the one about people sitting in separate sections of the bus **have become** illegal **since Rosa Parks refused to change her seat.** [3]The federal government **has not allowed** those laws **for over forty years.**

Presentation

Questions

1. What form of the verb do you see in sentences 1 and 3?

2. What is the time in sentence 1? (When did laws start to change?) What is the time in sentence 3?

3. What word or words follow *since* in sentences 1 and 2? Is the meaning of *since* the same in both sentences? How are these two ways of using *since* different?

Explanation—Present Perfect: From Past to Present with *For/Since*

1. Sometimes present perfect verb forms give information about actions or states that started in the past, continue to the present, and may even continue into the future.
2. You will often find these forms with the words *for* and *since*. These words indicate that something started in the past and continues until now.

   • *for* = amount of time (how long/duration)

   Laws about where to sit on a bus *have been* illegal *for many years*.
   The federal government *has not allowed* those laws *for over forty years*.

- *since* = starting time (when this action or state started)

Many Jim Crow laws *have changed since 1955.*

Many Jim Crow laws *have become* illegal *since Rosa Parks refused to change her seat.*

Notice that the start time after the word *since* could be a noun, or it could be an entire clause. *(Review subordinating conjunctions: Unit Two, page 45, item 7.)*

3. **Negative sentences**

RULE: Add the word *not* after the auxiliary to make a sentence negative. (See Lesson 8 for a review.)

Some laws *have not (haven't*) changed* since 1955.

The federal government *has not (hasn't*) allowed* those laws for over forty years.

4. **Questions**

RULE: Place the auxiliary to the left of the subject of the sentence. (See Lesson 8 for a review.)

Have some laws *changed* since 1956? *Why have some laws changed? Who has changed* some laws?

Practice

Activity 1 *(Review subordinating conjunction **since**: Unit Two, page 45.)*

Complete the sentences below with the present perfect form of the verb and circle the for *or* since *in parentheses to fit the sentence.*

1. (For/Since) the Civil War, Jim Crow laws (come) _____ and (go) _____.

2. Segregation in public schools (be) _____ illegal (for/since) several decades.

3. Many schools (integrate) _____ their classrooms (for/since) the Supreme Court ruled against segregated schools in 1954.

4. Non-white students (attend) _____ previously segregated schools (since/for) over 50 years now.

5. Many schools in the United States (see) _____ more diversity in their classrooms (since/for) 1954.

6. School systems (make) _____ these important changes (for/since) this famous Supreme Court decision.

_____
*Contractions are often used in conversation. They are not usually used in formal writing.

Activity 2

Find seven mistakes in the following conversation and show how to correct each one.

Helen: Hi, Jim. Where has you been for the last few days? You've missed some interesting discussions in history class.

Jim: I've had a cold for last weekend, but I am starting to feel better today. What exactly have I missed in class yesterday?

Helen: We talked about the *Brown vs. Board of Education* decision and how schools have integrate their classrooms since then.

Jim: Was the whole class about that?

Helen: No, we also discussed some things that have happen more recently in education. Did you know that since the past few years the focus in education have changed from integration to individual achievement?

Activity 3

A. *Using the information given under each line below, write questions about the Civil Rights Movement. Use the present perfect form of the verb in each question.*

1. _____
   how long / the idea of separate but equal / in the schools / be / unconstitutional

2. _____
   (yes/no question) the "I Have Dream Speech" / be / famous / for over 100 years

3. _____
   how long / this country / have / a federal civil rights law

B. *Complete each answer to the questions above in a complete sentence using the information on the timeline below. Use the present perfect form of the verb and either* for *or* since *in each of your answers.*

1954 Supreme Court rules "separate but equal" is unconstitutional
1963 Martin Luther King's "I Have a Dream" speech
1964 President Johnson signs the federal Civil Rights Act

1. The idea of "separate but equal" _____

2. The "I Have a Dream" speech _____

3. This country _____

Activity 4

Circle the answer in parentheses that is true for the meaning of each sentence below.

1. I *have been* a teacher for almost 30 years.

   I (am/am not) still a teacher.

2. Some students in this class *have taken* two history classes already.

   Some students (finished/did not finish) two history classes.

3. One of my teachers *has given* several tests this semester.

   The class (took/did not take) several tests this semester.

4. You *have known* about next week's test in that class for over two weeks.

   You (learned about/did not learn about) next week's test over two weeks ago.

5. My friend *has wanted* to learn more about U.S. history since he took History 205 last year.

   My friend (does/does not) want to learn more about U.S. history now.

6. We *have studied* U.S. history since last week in this class.

   We (finished/did not finish) studying U.S. history in this class.

7. I *have read* several books about the Civil Rights Movement in my classes.

   I (finished/did not finish) reading several books about the Civil Rights Movement.

8. Those students *have changed* schools three times in the last ten years.

   They (are continuing to change/they finished three changes to) schools.

Activity 5

A. *With a partner, write five questions to ask your classmates about their lives using the verbs below in present perfect form. You should begin each question with "How long."*

EXAMPLE: How long have you owned your car?

live	like	believe	be	see	know
take	make	have	own	speak	hear

1. _____

2. _____

3. _____

4. _____

5. _____

B. *Find a different partner and ask him/her your questions. Write your partner's answers in complete sentences using present perfect verb forms and* for *or* since.

1. _____

2. _____

3. _____

4. _____

5. _____

Present Perfect Progressive (Continuous*)

From Past to Present with For and Since

```
+----------------------------+------->
1954                          now
```
Brown vs. Board of Education case

[1]**Since the Supreme Court declared** the idea of "separate but equal" illegal in 1954, many schools **have been experiencing** changes. [2]These changes **have been taking** place **for several decades now.** [3]**What has been happening** in the schools **since that important decision?**

Presentation

Questions

1. What ending do you see on the verb in sentence 2? What helping verbs (auxiliaries) do you see with this verb?

2. What is the time in all of these sentences? How do you know?

3. How are the verb forms in bold the same as present perfect verbs, and how are they different?

Explanation—Present Perfect Progressive (Continuous*): From Past to Present with *For* and *Since*

1. **Regular verbs:** *have/has* + *been* + verb + *-ing*

    Be sure to have all four of these pieces, including the two auxiliaries *(have/be)* and the *-ing* ending.

    Many schools *have been implementing* changes since the Supreme
                       1   2   3   4
    Court decision in 1954.

2. **Negative sentences**

    RULE: Add the word *not* after the auxiliary to make a sentence negative. When there are two auxiliaries, place *not* after the first one.

---

*Note: Sometimes the word *continuous* is used in place of the word *progressive*. These words have the same meaning.

These changes *have not (haven't*) been taking* place in many areas for several decades.

That school *has not (hasn't*) been making* changes.

Follow this pattern for negative sentences using present perfect progressive verb forms:

subject	auxiliary *(have)*	*not*	*be* (past participle)	verb + *-ing*	
These changes	have	not	been	taking place	in many areas.
That school	has	not	been	making	changes.

3. **Questions**

   a. **Yes/no questions**

   RULE: Place the auxiliary to the left of the subject. When there are two auxiliaries, move only the first one.

   Have these changes *been taking place* for decades?

   Has that school *been making* changes?

Follow this pattern for yes/no questions with present perfect progressive verb forms:

auxiliary *(have)*	subject	*be* (past participle)	verb + *-ing*	
Have	these changes	been	taking place	for decades?
Has	that school	been	making	changes?

   b. **Question word questions**

   RULE: Add the question word and place the first auxiliary to the left of the subject.

   Why have they *been making* changes? *What changes has* that school *been making? Who has been making* changes? *Which rules have been changing?*

Follow this pattern for question word questions with present perfect progressive verb forms:

question word	auxiliary *(have)*	subject	*be* (past participle)	verb + *-ing*	
Why	have	they	been	making	changes?
What changes	has	that school	been	making?	
Who	has		been	making	changes?
Which rules	have		been	changing?	

---

*Contractions are often used in conversation. They are not usually used in formal writing.

4. Use these verb forms for actions/events that started in the past, continue until now, and may continue into the future.

    Do not use these forms for stative (non-action) verbs. (See Lesson 4, page 24 to review stative verbs.)

5. Native speakers use the present perfect progressive form for actions that started in the past and continue until now more often than the present perfect form (unless the verb is stative).

    > We *have been making* changes for decades in the schools. These changes *have not been* easy through the years.

6. There are a few verbs that can be used in both the present perfect and present perfect progressive forms without a difference in meaning.

    These verbs include: *live, work, teach, study, stay,* and *wear.*

    > She *has lived* in that city since she was born. She *has been living* in that city since she was born.

Activity 1

Read each sentence below and decide if the information that follows each one is true (T) or false (F).

1. Many schools have been working on problems related to diversity in the classroom.

    _____ Those schools are no longer working on those problems.

2. I've read many articles in magazines and on the Internet about those problems in the schools.

    _____ I am still reading those articles because I did not finish them.

3. I've visited schools in my neighborhood with those problems.

    _____ I completed some visits to those schools already.

4. My friend's children have been attending private school for several years now.

    _____ My friend's children are still attending private school today.

5. My neighbor and I have both been living on the same street for many years.

    _____ My neighbor is new to this street.

Activity 2

Fill in the spaces with the present perfect progressive form of a verb from the list below. Use a different verb for each sentence.

face	struggle	try	make

1. For over 50 years now many schools in the United States

    _____ with difficult issues in education.

2. Educators across the United States _____ to provide a

    quality education for all students.

3. Many schools _____ efforts to address linguistic and

    cultural diversity in the classroom.

4. Therefore, educators _____ language issues as well as

    integration issues.

Activity 3

Circle the correct verb form in parentheses. Then answer the questions that follow as true (T) or false (F).

Stan: Hi, Amy. What (are you doing/have you done/have you been doing) for the past few days? I (haven't seen/didn't see/haven't been seeing) you since last Monday.

Amy: I (have been/has been/have been being) in the library for over three hours a day since Sunday for an assignment about school integration.

Stan: Why (you have been working/have you been working/have you worked) so hard on that? Is it a new assignment?

Amy: No, I (have know/have known/have been knowing) about it since the first week of the semester, but I (haven't had/haven't been having/haven't have) time to work on it very much until recently.

Stan: I know what you mean. I have a big assignment too. I (have be researching/have been research/have been researching) information for it since last month. I still (haven't finished/haven't finish/not have finished) everything yet. Maybe I'll see you in the library some time.

_____ 1. Amy and Stan have seen each other several times from Monday until now.

_____ 2. Amy went to the library for three hours on one day only.

_____ 3. The teacher gave the assignment to Amy's class when the class first met.

_____ 4. Amy has been very busy, so she couldn't work on the assignment before this week.

_____ 5. Stan finished the research for his assignment.

Activity 4

Read each situation below and write a question using the present perfect progressive form of the verb and the question word. Then write the answer to the question using the present perfect progressive form of the verb and the other information in parentheses.

1. You are meeting a friend at the library today. You agreed to meet at 2:00 PM, and it is now 2:30 PM Your friend is just arriving. What will you ask your friend and what will she/he answer?

    (what/do) _____ ?

    (look for)_____

2. You need to speak with your friend about something important. However, for the last hour nobody has answered the phone. Finally, she has just picked up the phone.

    (why/answer/negative) _____ ?

    (study with headphones)_____

3. You are just leaving the library, and you run into a classmate you haven't seen since last semester. What will you ask about school this semester?

    (which classes/take)_____ ?

    (study)_____

Activity 5

Fill in the spaces with the correct form of the verb in parentheses. Try to use each one of the following verb forms at least once. More than one verb tense may be appropriate for some sentences.

simple past	past progressive
present perfect	present perfect progressive

On November 14, 1960, a six-year-old girl named Ruby Bridges (walk) _____ to the William Frantz Public School in New Orleans
1
as the first black child to integrate it. Four U.S. marshals (accompany) _____ her because there (be) _____ a large crowd of
2   3
angry people at the school, and the people (protest) _____ against
4
integration. The parents of the children in her class (take) _____
5
their children out of that school, so Ruby (become) _____ the only
6
student in the class with her teacher Barbara Henry that year.

In 1995 Ruby Bridges and Barbara Henry (see) _____
7
each other again for the first time in many years. Since then they (stay) _____ in touch with each other. They (visit) _____
8   9
schools and teacher conferences around the country in order to talk about racism and education today. For the past several years Ruby Bridges (speak) _____ to school children about her experiences in the
10
hopes that teaching children will help prevent racism in the future. She (write—also) _____ her story in the book *Through My Eyes,* and
11
she (start—recently) _____ a foundation called Ruby's Bridges to
12
work with diverse student populations in schools across the country.

Activity 6

A. Fill in this timeline about your life, using some of the verbs below. Add specific years to the line. Think of things that started in the past and continue until today. Put any of the verbs below that fit your life in the appropriate places on the line. If you can think of other verbs related to things in your life, put those on the line as well.

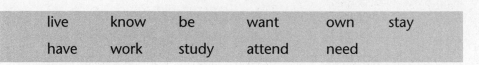

year of birth   present

| live | know | be | want | own | stay |
| have | work | study | attend | need | |

Now write sentences about your life using the information from the timeline above. Be sure to use present perfect and present perfect progressive forms of the verbs as well as for and since in your sentences. Discuss this information with a partner.

_____

_____

_____

_____

_____

B. Write some of the information you learned about your partner in a short paragraph.

_____

_____

_____

_____

_____

_____

Past Perfect

[1]Thurgood Marshall became the first African-American Supreme Court Justice in 1987. [2]Before that he **had argued** many cases at the United States Supreme Court as legal counsel for various people and organizations. [3]After he **had won** 14 cases in that court, he became a Supreme Court Justice.

Presentation

Questions

1. What form of the verb do you see in sentence 1? What is the time of this sentence?

2. What ending do you see on the verb in bold in sentence 2? What helping verb (auxiliary) do you see with the verbs in bold in sentences 2 and 3?

3. How many clauses and verbs do you see in sentence 3? What is the time of this sentence? Which of these two actions do you think finished first?

Explanation—Past Perfect

1. *Had* + verb (past participle)

    Before 1987 Thurgood Marshall *had argued* many cases at the Supreme Court. After he *had won* 14 cases in that court, he *became* a Supreme Court Justice.

2. Negative sentences

    RULE: Add the word *not* after the auxiliary to make a sentence negative.

    He *had not (hadn't*) argued* many important cases before he became a Supreme Court Justice.

    Other black lawyers *had not (hadn't*) argued* cases at the Supreme Court before that time.

---

*Contractions are often used in conversation. They are not usually used in formal writing.

Follow this pattern for negative sentences with past perfect verb forms:

subject	auxiliary	not	verb (past participle)	
He	had	not	argued	many important cases . . .
Other black lawyers	had	not	argued	cases . . .

3. **Questions**

   RULE: Place the auxiliary to the left of the subject of the sentence.

   a. **Yes/no questions**

   Had he *argued* many cases before he became a Supreme Court Justice?

   Had other lawyers *argued* as many cases at the Supreme Court before that time?

Follow this pattern for yes/no questions with past perfect verb forms:

auxiliary	subject	verb (past participle)	
Had	he	argued	many cases . . . ?
Had	other lawyers	argued	as many cases . . . ?

   b. **Question word questions**

   Place the question word and the auxiliary to the left of the subject.

   Where had he *argued* other cases before he became a Supreme Court Justice?

   What kinds of cases *had* other lawyers *argued* before that time?

   Who had argued other cases before that time?

Follow this pattern for question word questions with past perfect verb forms:

question word	auxiliary	subject	verb (past participle)	
Where	had	he	argued	other cases . . . ?
What kinds of cases	had	other lawyers	argued	before that time?
Who	had		argued	other cases . . . ?

4. Use the past perfect tense when you want to show a relationship between two events or actions in the past. Use the past perfect verb form (*had* + past participle) to indicate the event that finished first or before a specific time.

   a. *Before 1987* Thurgood Marshall *had argued* many cases in the Supreme Court.

   Which happened first: 1987 or he argued many cases?

   argued many cases   1987

b. After he *had won* 14 cases in that court, he *became* a Supreme Court Justice.

Which happened first: he won 14 cases or he became a Supreme Court Justice?

1987

won 14 cases   became Supreme Court Justice

NOTE: Native speakers may not use past perfect verb forms in conversation or in informal English. Instead, they may use two simple past verbs.

He *won* many cases before he *became* a Supreme Court Justice.

5. Remember that past perfect refers to two things in the past. The action or event that finished first is past perfect, and the second action or event is simple past.

Do not use the past perfect form for one event in the past with no relationship to another event or time.

INCORRECT: Yesterday we ~~had~~ learned about the Civil War in history class.

CORRECT: We *had learned* about the Civil War before we *studied* about Jim Crow laws.

Do not use past perfect verb forms in both clauses of a sentence. Past perfect indicates the earlier event, so only one verb should show this.

INCORRECT: We had learned about the Civil War before we ~~had~~ studied about Jim Crow laws.

6. You may see the words *by* or *by the time* used with past perfect verb forms. These words indicate an end time, so the action or event before it may be in past perfect form. These time expressions marking a specific time or date often appear at the beginning or end of a statement.

By 1987 Thurgood Marshall *had argued* many cases at the Supreme Court.

You may also see adverbs such as *already* and *just* with past perfect verb forms. Note that the adverbs *just* and *already* are placed between the auxiliary and the verb.

By the time Thurgood Marshall became a Supreme Court Justice, he *had already won* many cases in that court.

We *had just won* a case when we heard about his appointment.

Practice

Activity 1

Read the following sentences about Jim Crow laws and indicate which action or event finished first with a number 1 and which one was second with a number 2.

EXAMPLE:

Before Jim Crow laws became popular, African-Americans had enjoyed some new freedoms.

__2__ Jim Crow laws became popular.

__1__ African-Americans enjoyed some new freedoms.

1. By the 1890s whites in the north had become less supportive of civil rights issues.

   _____ Whites became less supportive.

   _____ the 1890s

2. Before the Supreme Court decision in 1954 about segregation in schools, another case in 1896 had established the idea of "separate but equal."

   _____ The Supreme Court made a decision in 1954.

   _____ Another case in 1896 established "separate but equal."

3. After many people had suffered under Jim Crow laws for years, over 200,000 people marched on Washington, D.C. in 1963 with Martin Luther King, Jr.

   _____ 200,000 people marched on Washington, D.C.

   _____ Many people suffered under Jim Crow laws.

4. Jim Crow laws occurred because the Civil War had not solved racial problems in the United States.

   _____ The Civil War didn't solve racial problems.

   _____ Jim Crow laws occurred.

Activity 2   *(Review subordinating conjunctions: Unit Two, pages 42–49.)*

A.   *Fill in the blanks with the past perfect form of the verb given.*

1. Thurgood Marshall's great-grandfather (be) _____ a slave before he became a free man.

2. Because he (remain—negative) _____ a slave, he was able to marry a white woman and live away from the plantation .

3. Thurgood Marshall (attend) _____ segregated schools before he went to college.

4. Thurgood Marshall attended Lincoln University after his brother (graduate—already) _____ from that school.

5. By 1930 Thurgood Marshall (finish) _____ college.

B.   *Fill in the blanks with the simple past or past perfect of the verb given.*

1. Thurgood Marshall (apply) _____ to the University of Maryland law school before he (graduate) _____ college.

2. After the University of Maryland (refuse) _____ him entry because of its segregated policies, he (go) _____ to law school at Howard University.

3. He (establish) _____ his law practice after he (passed) _____ the bar exam.

4. By 1938 he (become) _____ the chief lawyer for an organization called the National Association for the Advancement of Colored People, or NAACP.

5. Before he (leave) _____ the NAACP, he (take charge of) _____ all of its legal matters.

Activity 3 *(Review subordinating conjunctions: Unit Two, pages 42–49.)*

Find ten mistakes in the following paragraph and show how to fix them.

Mary McLeod Bethune was born in 1875. Her parents have been slaves before the end of the Civil War. Mary was fortunate because she has been able to get an education as a young girl. Before that, she had want to become a missionary in Africa. However, later she had decided to help African-Americans in her own country. After she taught school in Georgia, she taught in South Carolina, Florida, and Illinois. By 1904, with only $1.50, she was opened a school called The Daytona Normal and Industrial Institute for Negro Girls. The school opened with five girls and the tuition was 50 cents a week. However, Mary had never refused to educate any child because of money problems. By the time she left her position as president of the school, she was there for more than 40 years. Mary was the first African-American woman to be involved with advising various U.S. presidents. Before she had died in 1955, four different presidents called on her for help with several projects regarding youth and education.

Activity 4

Write sentences about the life of Maya Angelou using the timeline below and a verb in the past perfect tense in each sentence. Use the words given in parentheses for four sentences. Then write two more sentences on your own. Try to use the words already *and* just *in some sentences as well.*

- born in 1928
- as a young child lived in small segregated town with her grandmother in Arkansas
- at 7 years old sent to live with her mother in St. Louis, Missouri
- returned to Arkansas; met an influential teacher and learned about literature
- 1950s studied to be a dancer
- worked as an educator in Cairo
- taught music and drama in Ghana
- 1970 became famous for her first book *(I Know Why the Caged Bird Sings)*
- 1977 nominated for an Emmy Award for acting in "Roots"
- 1993 read her poem "On the Pulse of Morning" for President Bill Clinton's inauguration

1. (after—two clauses) _____

_____

2. (by the1950s—one clause) _____

_____

3. (before—two clauses)_____

_____

4. (by the time—two clauses) _____

_____

5. _____

_____

6. _____

_____

Past Perfect Progressive (Continuous*)

[1]Jackie Robinson **had been playing** Negro League baseball before he joined the Brooklyn Dodgers. [2]After Dodger scouts **had been watching** various players, the team signed Jackie to play. [3]Non-white players **had not been participating** in major league baseball before 1947.

Presentation

Questions

1. What ending do you see on the verbs in bold in sentences 1 and 2? What helping verbs (auxiliaries) are with these verbs?

2. How many clauses are there in sentences 1 and 2? Which action do you think finished first?

3. Look at the verb in bold in sentence 3. What is the rule for making this verb form negative?

Explanation—Past Perfect Progressive (Continuous*)

1. regular verbs: *had + been + verb + -ing*

   Be sure to have all four of these pieces, including the two auxiliaries *(have/be)* and the *-ing* ending.

   Jackie Robinson **had been playing** Negro League baseball before he
   1   2   3   4

   joined the Dodgers.

2. **Negative sentences**

   RULE: Add the word *not* after the **first** auxiliary to make a sentence negative.

---

*Note: Sometimes the word *continuous* is used in place of the word *progressive*. These words have the same meaning.

Jackie Robinson *had not (hadn't*) been playing* in the Negro League before he joined the Dodgers.

Non-white players *had not (hadn't*) been participating* in major league baseball before 1947.

Follow this pattern for negative sentences using past perfect progressive verb forms:

subject	auxiliary (have)	not	be (past participle)	verb + -ing	
Jackie Robinson	had	not	been	playing	in the Negro . . .
Non-white players	had	not	been	participating	in major league . . .

3. **Questions**

   a. **Yes/no questions**

   RULE: Place the **first** auxiliary to the left of the subject.

   Had non-white players *been participating* in major league baseball before 1947?

   Had Jackie Robinson *been playing* in the Negro League before he joined the Dodgers?

Follow this pattern for yes/no questions with past perfect progressive verb forms:

auxiliary (have)	subject	be (past participle)	verb + -ing	
Had	non-white players	been	participating	in major league . . . ?
Had	Jackie Robinson	been	playing	in the Negro league . . . ?

   b. **Question word questions**

   RULE: Add the question word and place the **first** auxiliary to the left of the subject.

   Why had they been keeping segregated baseball leagues before 1947?

   Where had the Dodger scouts *been watching* Jackie Robinson before they signed him to play?

   Who had been playing in the Negro league?

Follow this pattern for question word questions with past perfect progressive verb forms:

question word	auxiliary (have)	subject	be (past participle)	verb + -ing	
Why	had	they	been	keeping	segregated . . . ?
Where	had	the Dodgers	been	watching	Jackie . . . ?
Who	had		been	playing	in the . . .

---

*Contractions are often used in conversation. They are not usually used in formal writing.

4. Past perfect progressive verb forms work in much the same way as past perfect verb forms because the past perfect progressive indicates something finished before another event or situation in the past. However, the progressive indicates a longer period of time or duration. Therefore, the event or action that finished first was in progress for a long time before it finished.

> Non-white baseball players *had been participating* in a separate league before 1947.
>
> Which happened first? The year 1947 or non-white players playing in a separate league?

participating in a separate league   1947

Do not use these forms for stative (non-action) verbs. Stative verbs can be in past perfect form but not past perfect progressive. (See Lesson 4, page 24 to review stative verbs.)

> CORRECT: Jackie Robinson had known about the difficulties of integrating the team before he became a Dodger.
>
> INCORRECT: Jackie Robinson ~~had been knowing~~ about the difficulties of integrating the team before he became a Dodger.

Practice

Activity 1   (*Review subordinating conjunctions: Unit Two, pages 42–49.*)

A. *Fill in the blanks with the past perfect progressive form of the verbs given below. Use each verb only one time. (Some verbs may fit more than one sentence.)*

play	attend	live	compete	excel

1. As a child Jackie Robinson _____ in Georgia before his mother moved the family to California.

2. He _____ UCLA for three years when he quit to help support his family.

3. By the time he left UCLA, he _____ in four different sports there.

4. Before Jackie Robinson became a Dodger, black and white baseball players _____ in separate leagues.

5. Jackie Robinson joined the Brooklyn Dodgers after he _____ on a team called the Kansas City Monarchs.

B. *Fill in the blanks with the simple past or past perfect progressive form of the verb given. Use any other words given in parentheses as well.*

1. When Jackie Robinson (become) _____ a Dodger, some people (already—fight) _____ against segregation in that sport.

2. Before 1947 various civil rights organizations (put) _____ pressure on major league baseball teams to integrate.

3. Before the Dodgers (consider) _____ inviting Robinson to join the team, Jackie and the Dodgers' manager (discuss) _____ the difficulties of the situation.

4. Even after some other major league teams (talk) _____ about a boycott to protest Robinson's presence in the league, the Dodgers (sign) _____ him.

5. By the time Jackie Robinson (leave) _____ the Dodgers, other black players (play) _____ in the major league teams as well.

Activity 2   *(Review coordinating and subordinating conjunctions: Unit One, pages 8–13 and Unit 2, pages 42–49.)*

Choose the form of the verb in parentheses that best completes each sentence in the following story about Oprah Winfrey. Then answer the questions that follow.

Oprah Winfrey (spent/had been spending) her first three years on a farm in Mississippi with her grandmother. By the time she (had been/was) three, she (learned/had already learned) to read and (performed/had been performing) recitations. At age six she (moved/had been moving) to Milwaukee, Wisconsin to live with her mother. However, life (had been/was) difficult there. Before she (had turned/turned) 13 years old, she (had run/had been running) away from home, so her family sent her to live in Nashville, Tennessee with her strict father. At age 17, Oprah (had begun/began) a broadcasting career in radio in Nashville. By the time she (agreed/had been agreeing) to be a co-host of a talk show in Baltimore, she (had already been working/worked) as a news anchor there. In 1984 she (had been coming/came) to Chicago to host a failing talk show. By the end of her first year there, she (created/had created) a very popular show. Later, she also (formed/had been forming) her own private production company, named Harpo Productions, Inc., and this company now owns her talk show. No woman (had ever owned/had ever been owning) her own talk show before Oprah. In addition, by 1983 Oprah (had become/had been becoming) the first African-American woman billionaire.

Questions

Indicate true (T) *or false* (F) *according to the story about Oprah Winfrey.*

_____ 1. Oprah learned to read after she was three years old.

_____ 2. Oprah ran away from home after she moved to Nashville, Tennessee to live with her father.

_____ 3. Oprah started a job as a radio broadcaster after she moved in with her father.

_____ 4. Oprah worked as a news show anchor before she became a talk show host.

_____ 5. It took Oprah more than a year to make her talk show a success.

_____ 6. Oprah became the first woman to own her own talk show.

Activity 3   *(Review subordinating conjunctions: Unit Two, pages 42–49.)*

Find nine mistakes in the following paragraph and show how to fix them.

In 1995 an 87-year-old laundry woman named Oseola McCarty took a train from Hattiesburg, Mississippi to Washington, D.C. for a dinner ceremony in her honor with President Clinton. What had she did to receive this honor? Her gift of $150,000 in scholarship money to the University of Southern Mississippi was the reason. She had be saving her earnings for many years before she donated this large gift. In fact, she had been wash and iron other people's clothes for 75 years before she finally stopped working. How could she save so much money from that job?

After she had been dropping out of school in the sixth grade, she started to work and put her money in a savings account at a bank. She also had living frugally since her childhood in order to save more money. People at the bank had realized that she had been accumulating a sizeable amount of money. Therefore, they advised her to invest it in some other accounts.

She told the people at the bank she had be thinking about what to do with the money for a long time. Finally by 1995 she had been saved enough money to establish a scholarship in her name.

Activity 4   *(Review subordinating conjunctions: Unit Two, pages 42–49.)*

Look at the following timeline about the life of Dr. Martin Luther King, Jr. and complete both Part A and Part B below.

1955	led the boycott of segregated buses in Montgomery, Alabama and gained national attention
1957	formed a group called Southern Christian Leadership Conference to fight segregation
1959	visited India to study Mahatma Gandhi's philosophy of nonviolence
1963	led a march of over 200,000 people in Washington, D.C.; made his famous "I Have a Dream" speech at this civil rights demonstration
1964	awarded a Nobel Peace Prize
1967	announced the beginning of a "Poor People's Campaign" focusing on jobs and freedom for poor people
1968	marched in Memphis, Tennessee to support a strike of the sanitation workers there; was shot and killed in Memphis, Tennessee

A. *Complete each sentence with a complete clause that includes information from the timeline. You should use a past perfect or past perfect progressive form of a verb in your answer.*

1. By 1959, Dr. Martin Luther King had already _____

    _____ .

2. Before Dr. King led the march on Washington, he had _____

    _____ .

3. Dr. King was awarded the Nobel Peace Prize after he had _____

    _____ .

4. By the time Dr. King died, he had _____

    _____ .

B. *Answer the following questions in complete sentences using the information about Dr. King.*

1. In general, what kind of work had Dr. King been doing before he went to India?

    _____

    _____

2. What work had he been doing just before he was shot and killed?

    _____

    _____

3. By the time he died, had he won any awards?

    _____

    _____

Activity 5

A. *Create a short timeline of at least four or five dates and events in your own life. Then write two sentences about the dates and events on this timeline using the past perfect verb form and write two sentences using the past perfect progressive verb form.*

    _____

    _____

    _____

    _____

    _____

B. *Work with a partner and read each other your sentences from Part A. Write a short paragraph about what you learned about your partner.*

    _____

    _____

    _____

    _____

    _____

    _____

INTRODUCTION TO MODALS

As discussed in the introduction to verbs and auxiliaries, one group of auxiliaries is called *modals*. The nine modals in English are:

can   could   may   might   should
will   would   must   shall

1. These words all have different meanings and can be used in different situations as you will see in Unit Three.
2. All nine modals follow some rules of grammar that do not change.

RULE 1: Do not add an ending to a modal.

> **Correct:**   She **can speak** three languages.
>
> **Incorrect:**   She **cans speak** three languages.

RULE 2: Do not add an ending to the verb after a modal.

> **Correct:**   She can **speak** three languages.
>
> **Incorrect:**   She can **speaks** three languages.

RULE 3: Do not add the word "to" between a modal and a verb.

> **Correct:**   We **might go** to the movies today.
>
> **Incorrect:**   We might **to** go to the movies today.

RULE 4: Do not use more than one modal in a sequence (next to each other).

> **Correct:**   They **must pay** their rent today.
>
> **Incorrect:**   They must **might** pay their rent today.

3. There are some two- and three-word expressions that have the same meanings as the modals. However, these expressions do not follow all of the same grammar rules as the modals. Some people call these *equivalent expressions* or *semi-modals*.

    Following are some of these expressions that you will learn about in Unit Three.

    be able to = can/could   *have to = must*
    ought to = should   *have got to = must*
    had better = (strong) should

Ability

Can/Could/Be Able To

[1]Several factors affect our health. [2]We **can change** some of them, such as lifestyle and environment. [3]Others, such as genetic factors, we **are not able to change**. [4]In the past we **could change even fewer factors**.

Presentation

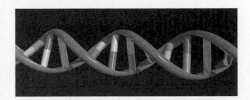

Questions

1. Look at the words in bold that come before the verb *change* in each sentence. What is the meaning of these words?

2. What is the time in sentences 2 and 3? What is the time in sentence 4?

3. How is the grammar of the words in bold in sentence 3 different from the grammar of the words in bold in sentences 2 and 4?

Explanation—*Can/Could/Be Able To*

1. The following modals and equivalent expression express ability in English:

   can   could   be able to

2. Modals *(can/could)* do not add tense endings and do not change to agree with the subject. (See page 91.) However, *be able to* makes these changes.

   We *can change* our lifestyle. He *could change* his environment.
   We *are (we're*) able to change* our lifestyle. He *was able to change* his environment.

---

*Contractions are often used in conversation. They are not usually used in formal writing.

3. **Negative sentences**

   RULE: Add the word *not* after the auxiliary.

   We *cannot* (can't†) change* some things.

Follow this pattern for negative sentences using *can, could,* and *be able to:*

subject	auxiliary	not	verb (simple form) or *able to* + verb	
We	can	not	change	some things.
He	could	not	change	some things.
She	was (is)	not	able to change	things.

4. **Questions**

   a. **Yes/no questions**

   RULE: Place the auxiliary to the left of the subject of the sentence.

   Can he change his lifestyle? *Could* she change her lifestyle?

Follow this pattern for yes/no questions using *can, could,* and *be able to:*

auxiliary	subject	verb (simple form) or *able to* + verb	
Can	he	change	his lifestyle?
Could	she	change	her lifestyle?
Are / Were	you	able to change	your lifestyle?
Were	you	able to change	your lifestyle?

   b. **Question word questions**

   RULE: Place the question word and the auxiliary to the left of the subject.

   When can your lifestyle *affect* your health? *Why could* she live a healthier lifestyle in the past? *How were* you *able to change* your lifestyle?

Follow this pattern for question word questions using *can, could,* and *be able to:*

question word	auxiliary	subject	verb (simple form) or *be able to* + verb	
When	can	your lifestyle	affect	your health?
Why	could	she	live	a healthier lifestyle?
How	were	you	able to change	your lifestyle?

---

*Can + *not* is written as *cannot*. It is the only modal that joins in this way.
†Contractions are often used in conversation. They are not usually used in formal writing.

5. We use both *could* and *be able to* in different time frames, such as past, present, and future. However, do not use *can* in the past.

    CORRECT: In the past *we could change* fewer things about our environment.

    In the past we *were able to change* fewer things about our environment.

    In the future we *will be able to change* even more things in our environment.

    INCORRECT: In the past we *can change* fewer things about our environment.

    In addition, we use *could* for past ability when we are talking about something that was true in general in the past. We do not use it for something that was true for one time only.

    CORRECT: I *could change* some things about my lifestyle when I was younger.

    INCORRECT: Yesterday I *could start* my new diet.

Practice

Activity 1   *(Review transitions: Unit Three, pages 77–85.)*

A. *Fill in the blanks with either* can *or* could *and one of the verbs given. Make the sentence negative where indicated. In some cases more than one verb may fit the meaning of the sentence, but you should try to use each verb only one time.*

achieve   alter   make   ensure   change

In general, we (negative) _____ biological factors affecting our

                                1

health. In other words, our inherited factors are crucial to our health and

longevity. These days some people feel they _____ the aging

                                        2

process by changing how they look. For example, they _____ a

                                                3

younger look through procedures such as facelifts and silicone or botox

injections. In the past, some people thought they _____ these

                                                      4

changes through eating or drinking certain things, such as teas. However,

they (negative) _____ the same youthful looks that people can

                              5

today with the more advanced medical procedures.

B. *Fill in the blanks using* be able to *and the verb given in parentheses. Make the sentence negative where indicated and be sure to make any changes to fit the subject and the time of the sentence.*

Some people think that individuals (affect—negative) _____ the environment or help with any of the problems affecting our health. My friend George does not agree with this. Therefore, he joined a community organization, and a few months ago he (begin) _____ helping with some environmental projects in his town. For example, last month George and the other volunteers (work) _____ with city agencies to clean up a local park and the river that runs through it. In addition, his organization (help) _____ pass a new city ordinance about excessive noise a few weeks ago. George hopes in the future he (continue) _____ to help in this way. He feels strongly that individuals often (make) _____ changes on a local level; thus, he (envision) _____ a cleaner and safer environment through citizen-led efforts.

Activity 2   *(Review transitions: Unit Three, pages 77–85.)*

Find six mistakes in the following paragraph and show how to correct each one.

Kelly decided to make some lifestyle changes because she realizes she can improves her health by making some small modifications. For instance, she decided she could to limit the amount of caffeine she drinks, so last week she was able limit her coffee intake to one cup on the morning. At the same time she were able to eat fewer sweets and prepare more healthy snacks for herself. For example, last weekend she can prepare some trail mix and fruit mixes to eat instead of just grabbing her usual chocolate candy snacks. Now she is trying to convince her friend that she can does the same.

Activity 3

Using the information given under each line below, write a question using can, could, *or* be able to. *On the line below the words, write an answer using* can, could, *or* be able to *and the words given. Do not use the same word or expression for ability in both the question and answer.*

EXAMPLE:

Question: *Can people (Are people able to) make healthy lifestyle changes?*

(yes/no question)   people / make / healthy lifestyle changes

Answer: *Some people can (are able to) make those kinds of changes.*

some people/make/those kinds of changes

1. _____?

   (yes/no question)   we / change / genetic factors / about our health

   _____

   (negative)   we / alter / our inherited characteristics

2. _____?

   (yes/no question)   all people / find / good health care

   _____

   (negative)   many people / obtain / necessary basic health care

3. _____?

   how / public health workers / improve / the health of a community

   _____

   they / respond / to community problems / through disease prevention

4. _____?

   (yes/no question)   public health workers / help /
   many different people in the community

   _____

   they / address / community-wide problems /
   including everyone's health issues

5. _____?

   (yes/no question)   poor and homeless people /
   also benefit from public health care

   _____

   public health workers / assist /
   with issues of illness and poor housing conditions

6. _____?

   in what way / health care workers / work with the homeless /
   in your town / last year

   _____

   they / find out about / communicable diseases there /
   and helped stop them from spreading

7. _____ ?

   (yes/no question)   health care workers / help /
                       with housing last year as well

   _____

   they / contribute to the establishment of /
   some shelters for the cold winter months

Activity 4   *(Review transitions: Unit Three, pages 77–85.)*

A. *With a partner talk about improvements in health care and medicine between the past and today. First, think about the items on the following list; then, try to think about others as well.*

   • new vaccines for disease prevention

   • curing diseases (such as tuberculosis)

   • performing transplants (such as heart or liver)

   • using antibiotics for infections and diseases

B. *Write three to five sentences about what people could not do in the past, using* could *and* be able to.

   EXAMPLE:

   In the past we *could not (were not able to)* cure tuberculosis.

   _____

   _____

   _____

   _____

   _____

C. *After you write these sentences, change them to the present and make them positive.*

   EXAMPLE:

   Today we *can (are able to)* cure tuberculosis.

   Share all of your answers with the other students in the class.

   _____

   _____

   _____

   _____

   _____

Suggestions/Recommendations/Advice

Should/Ought To/Had Better/Might/Could

¹Richard **should get** some medicine for the pain. ²Perhaps he **ought to see** a doctor first. ³He **had better take** care of the problem, so it doesn't become chronic.

Presentation 1

Questions

1. Look at all the words in bold before the verbs in these sentences. Do they all have the same meaning?

2. How is the grammar the same or different for the words in bold in these sentences?

Explanation—*Should/Ought To/Had Better*

1. There are several words or expressions you can use to make recommendations/suggestions or to give advice.

   MODAL: should

   EQUIVALENT EXPRESSIONS: ought to   had better

2. The modal *should* follows the grammar rules for all modals. (See page 91.)

   She *should see* a doctor. He *should take* something for the pain.

3. *Ought to* and *had better* also come before the verb and do not change form or add endings. The verb following these expressions does not change form or add endings as well.

   She *ought to see* a doctor. They *ought to get* some medicine.

   She *had (She'd*) better take care of* the problem. She *had (She'd*) better be* careful about injuring it again.

   NOTE: In conversation, *ought to* may sound like *oughtta*. You should never write this form, but you will hear native speakers use it in conversation.

---

*Contractions are often used in conversation. They are not usually used in formal writing.

4. **Negative sentences**

   RULE: Add the word *not* after the auxiliary.

   a. You *should not (shouldn't*) see* a doctor. She *should not (shouldn't*)* take something for the pain.

   Follow this pattern for negative sentences using *should:*

subject	auxiliary	*not*	verb (simple form)	
You	should	not	see	a doctor.
She	should	not	take	something for the pain.

   b. To make a negative sentence with *had better,* add *not* after the expression.

   She *had better not exercise* too much. You *had better not go* to work if you are very sick.

   Follow this pattern for negative sentences using *had better:*

subject	*had better*	*not*	verb (simple form)	
She	had better	not	exercise	too much.
You	had better	not	go	to work . . .

   We do not usually use *ought to* in negative statements.

5. **Questions**

   a. **Yes/no questions**

   Usually we only use *should* in questions about advice or suggestions, not *had better* or *ought to.*

   RULE: Place the auxiliary to the left of the subject of the sentence.

   Should she *see* a doctor? *Should* I *take* some medicine for the pain?

   Follow this pattern for yes/no questions using *should:*

auxiliary	subject	verb (simple form)	
Should	she	see	a doctor?
Should	I	take	some medicine for the pain?

---

*Contractions are often used in conversation. They are not usually used in formal writing.

b. **Question word questions**

Place the question word and the auxiliary to the left of the subject.

Why should she *go* to a doctor? *When should* she *take* some medicine?

Follow this pattern for question word questions using *should:*

question word	auxiliary	subject	verb (simple form)	
Why	should	she	go	to a doctor?
When	should	she	take	some medicine?

6. *Should, ought to,* and *had better* are all used for recommendations, suggestions, or advice.

Ought to is more common in British English than in American English. You may not hear it as much in everyday spoken English in the United States.

Had better is more informal than the other two terms and is used mainly in speech. Its meaning is a little stronger than *should,* and it can sound like a threat. In other words, if you don't take this advice, something bad might happen.

EXAMPLE:

Your doctor says you *had better take* a certain medicine. (If you don't take it, there could be a problem, such as your condition could get worse.)

In the examples below, which one is more serious or a stronger recommendation?

You *should rest* for a couple of days to help your back.

You *had better get* some medicine for your back pain, or you won't be able to go to work.

NOTE: *Had better* looks like it is past time because *had* is the past form of *have.* However, we use *had better* for present, general, or future situations. We do not use it for past time. Look at the following examples:

You *had better be* careful about lifting things at work. (general time)

You *had better be* careful about lifting those boxes today. (present time)

You *had better be* careful about lifting any boxes in the next few days. (future time)

INCORRECT: You *had better be* careful about lifting the boxes yesterday.

Practice

Activity 1   *(Review transitions: Unit Three, pages 77–85.)*

Choose the correct word or expression in parentheses. Look carefully at the grammar around the word to make your choice.

In order to achieve and maintain good health, we (ought/had better) pay attention to four vital areas of our well-being: physical, mental, social, and spiritual. First, we (ought/should) to think about how to keep physically fit in order to have energy for daily necessary tasks, for leisure activities, and for emergencies. In addition, we (should/ought) not forget about the importance of our mental health. We (ought/had better) to work toward the highest level functioning of mental health that we possibly can. Next, we (ought/should) work toward having strong social support because strong family ties and friendships are likely to help people stay in good health. Finally, we (should to/ought to) try to develop some spirituality to help us find personal meaning in life and establish our personal goals. We (had better not/had not better) neglect any of these areas, for they all work together to help ensure our good health.

Activity 2

Find four mistakes in each of the following conversations and show how to fix them.

1. Betty: My son has a bad stomachache today. What I should give him for this?

   Carla: He ought try this herbal tea. It always works for my stomach problems.

   Betty: Really? How often should he takes it?

   Carla: You better read the instructions on the box. I can't remember.

2. Gary: I think I found a medicinal plant in my backyard.

   Steve: You had better to find out more about it before you try to use it as a remedy for something.

Gary: It looks just like the picture of a plant in my herb book. Why I should get more information?

Steve: Plant identification is often difficult. You have better find someone to help you with this. An expert ought to helps you make a more positive identification of it.

Activity 3   *(Review transitions: Unit Three, pages 77–85.)*

For each of the statements below write two sentences as follows:

   a. In the first sentence give advice using *should, ought to,* or *had better.*
   b. In the second sentence give advice using a negative and either *should* or *had better.*

1. I am starting to get a sore throat; also, I feel achy.

   You should (or ought to) go home and rest.

   You had better not work out at the gym today.

2. I have a terrible headache; furthermore, I have to teach a class in 15 minutes.

   _____

   _____

3. My mother is late for her doctor's appointment.

   _____

   _____

4. We can't understand the nurse's instructions about the medicine.

   _____

   _____

5. My friend just tripped and fell. He thinks he broke his foot.

   _____

   _____

6. This new medicine is not helping me; in other words, I'm still sick.

   _____

   _____

Presentation 2

Using *Could* and *Might* for Suggestions/Recommendations

Carol does not want to go to the doctor for her back pain. Her friend told her that she **could see** a chiropractor or she **might** just **rest** and wait a few days.

Questions

1. What is the meaning of the modals *could* and *might* in this presentation?

2. Do these words have exactly the same meaning as the words you learned at the beginning of this lesson *(should/ought to/had better)* ? How strong or weak in meaning do you think all of these words are?

Explanation—Could and *Might* for Recommendations

1. Use *could* and *might* when you want to make a suggestion that is mild or not too important. *Could* and *might* are not as strong as *should, ought to,* and *had better* when used for suggestions and recommendations.

   She *could see* a chiropractor. She *might rest* and wait a few days.

2. The modals *could* and *might* follow the grammar rules for all modals. (See page 91.)

3. We do not usually use *could* or *might* in negative sentences or in questions for this meaning of suggestion or recommendation. (See Lessons 14 and 17 for other meanings of these words and explanations for using them in negatives and questions for those meanings.)

Activity 4

Match each statement in the column on the left with the recommendation from the column on the right. Then label the following suggestions as strong (3), not too strong (2), or mild (weak) (1) in the space to the left of the number.

_____ 1. Joe has been coughing all day.

_____ 2. Ben's shoulder is sore from using one of the machines at the gym.

_____ 3. I haven't had a medical checkup in about two years.

_____ 4. The last time I saw the doctor my blood pressure was a little high.

_____ 5. Jim is having trouble getting to sleep these days.

_____ 6. I think I'm starting to get a cold.

_____ 7. I've had a bad rash for two days and it's getting worse.

a. You ought to make an appointment for one.

b. He might try to avoid drinking anything with caffeine in the evening.

c. You could have some chicken soup for dinner.

d. He might want to try a different machine the next time he goes there.

e. You'd better see a doctor and get some medicine for it.

f. You should check it again soon to see if it is still not right.

g. He had better not smoke any more cigarettes.

Activity 5

Complete each of the following sentences with appropriate suggestions or advice for each situation.

1. I think I'm getting a fever and my head hurts.

    You'd better _____

2. Bill is looking for a holistic doctor.

    He should _____

3. My stomachache is better, but I still feel a little sick.

    You might _____

4. I usually don't have time to cook; therefore, I eat a lot of junk food.

    You could _____

5. I hate to exercise, but I know it's good for my health.

    You ought to _____

Activity 6

With a partner or group write two or three suggestions or pieces of advice for each of the following situations. Each one should be a complete sentence using should, ought to, had better, could, *or* might. *Be sure to use each of these words or modal expressions at least once.*

1. Your friend smokes over a pack of cigarettes a day, and he wants to quit. Give him some advice/suggestions about how to do this.

    _____

    _____

    _____

    _____

    _____

2. Your brother is gaining weight and wants to change his diet to lose some weight. What advice can you give him about his eating habits?

    _____

    _____

    _____

    _____

    _____

3. A friend has been trying to lose weight but never does any exercise or physical activity. Make some suggestions about what she should do to help her lose weight.

    _____

    _____

    _____

    _____

    _____

4. Your mother has a very stressful job. Give her some advice or suggestions about what she can do when she is not working in order to relax and take away some of her stress.

    _____

    _____

    _____

    _____

    _____

Obligation/Necessity

Must/Have To/Have Got To

[1]Everyone **must follow** the rules at a medical office. [2]Each patient **has to sign in** with the receptionist and fill out all the papers. [3]Then all patients **have got to wait** for someone to call their names.

Presentation 1

Questions

1. What is the meaning of the words and expressions before the verbs in bold? How strong are these words?

2. How is the grammar of these expressions in sentences 2 and 3 different from the grammar of the modal *must* in sentence 1?

Explanation—*Must/Have To/Have Got To*

1. One modal and two equivalent expressions often express obligation or necessity in English:

   MODAL: must

   EXPRESSIONS (PHRASAL MODALS): have to   have got to

2. The modal *must* follows the grammar rules for all modals. (See page 91.)

   Everyone *must follow* the rules at a medical office. You *must wait* for someone to call your name.

3. The expressions *have to* and *have got to* also come before the verb. These expressions change to fit the sentence. The verb that follows them does not add any endings.

   They *have to sign* in at the reception desk. He *has to sign* in at the reception desk.

   We *have (We've*) got to* sign in at the reception desk. She *has (She's*) got to* sign in at the reception desk.

---

*Contractions are often used in conversation. They are not usually used in formal writing.

4. The expression *have to* can change with the time. It can be used with past, general, present, or future situations.

> I *have to make* an appointment with my doctor today.
>
> Yesterday he *had to call* the doctor's office early in the morning to get an appointment.
>
> She *will have to wait* until the morning to make her appointment because the office is closed.
>
> She *is going to have to wait* until the morning to make her appointment.

5. When *must* means obligation or necessity, we do not use it in the past. We use *had to* (the past of *have to*) to express past obligation or necessity. *Have got to* also doesn't change with time. It can be used only in the present.

> We *had to* sign in at the reception desk as soon as we got there.
>
> We *had to* wait for over 30 minutes to see the doctor yesterday.
>
> We *have got to* wait for the receptionist to call us.

6. **Questions**

We usually use *have to* for questions about obligation or necessity.

a. **Yes/no questions** with *have to*

To make yes/no questions with *have to,* place the auxiliary *do* before the subject.

> *Do* we *have to see* the receptionist at the desk?
>
> *Did* she *have to make* an appointment to see a doctor?

If the sentence is in the future, use the auxiliary *will* and not the auxiliary *do.*

> *Will* he *have to return* to the doctor tomorrow?

Follow this pattern for yes/no questions using *have to:*

auxiliary	subject	*have to* + verb	
Do	we	have to see	the receptionist at the desk?
Did	she	have to make	an appointment to see a doctor?
Will	he	have to return	to the doctor tomorrow?

b. **Question word questions** with *have to*

Place the question word and the auxiliary *do* to the left of the subject.

> *Why did* we *have to see* the receptionist first?
>
> *What does* she *have to do* at the reception desk?

If the sentence is in the future, use the auxiliary *will* and not the auxiliary *do.*

> *When will* he *have to return* to the doctor?

Follow this pattern for question word questions using *have to*:

question word	auxiliary	subject	*have to* + verb	
Why	did	we	have to see	the receptionist first?
What	does	she	have to do	at the reception desk?
When	will	he	have to return	to the doctor?

7. You may hear native speakers use *have to* and *have got to* more often than *must*. In conversation, you may hear the following short forms. You should never write these forms, but you will hear native speakers use them in conversation.

have to	You will hear *hafta*.	has to	You will hear *hasta*.
had to	You will hear *hadda*.	have got to	You will hear *gotta*.

Practice

Activity 1

A. *Fill in each space of the following rules at a doctor's office with one of the verbs below and the modal or expression in parentheses. Be sure to use the correct form of each of the words. Use each verb only one time.*

present   form   make   show   check in

1. Each patient (have to) _____ with the receptionist on arriving.

2. All patients (must) _____ a health plan card to the receptionist.

3. Every patient (have to) _____ a photo ID in addition to the card.

4. Patients (must) _____ a single line far enough behind the desk to ensure the privacy of others.

5. All patients (have got to) _____ any co-payment at check-in time.

B. *Change each of the sentences above into a yes/no question using* have to.

_____

_____

_____

_____

_____

_____

Activity 2

Find seven mistakes in the following conversation and show how to correct them.

Patient: Excuse me. We have been waiting for over half an hour, but nobody has called my son's name. We must to leave in half an hour for another appointment.

Receptionist: We're running late today. The doctor must take care of an emergency early this morning and this pushed back all his appointments.

Patient: My son have got to see the doctor as soon as possible. We really cannot wait.

Receptionist   I'm sorry, but you have got be a little patient with us. We are doing our best with the situation. I am afraid he will has to wait his turn.

Patient: We has to leave enough time to get to our next appointment. Can you please try to help?

Receptionist: Okay. I'll check with the nurse, but your son must waits here. I'll be right back.

Activity 3   *(Review transitions: Unit Three, pages 77–85.)*

Read the following situations and complete each sentence that follows with information about what the person needs to do. Use must, have to, *or* have got to *in each of your answers. Use each one at least once.*

1. Sandy needs a doctor's note for work because she is out sick today.

    Sandy _____

2. Mike's doctor told him to finish all of the prescribed medicine in the bottle.

    For the next ten days, Mike _____

3. There is a no smoking sign on the door of the hospital and Tom is getting ready to go in.

    Tom is smoking a cigarette; therefore, he _____

4. Yesterday, Barbara hurt her leg; as a result, she couldn't drive.

    In order to see a doctor yesterday, Barbara _____

5. Bob has been working ten hours a day; furthermore, now he is getting sick from the stress.

   Bob _____

6. Jane's doctor gave her new medicine for her blood pressure; in addition, she needs to see Jane again in two weeks.

   Jane _____

Presentation 2

Must and *Have To* in Negative Sentences

[1]When you see a Do Not Enter sign on a door, you **must find** another entrance.
[2]You **must not enter** through that door.
[3]Often at the doctor's office, you **have to wait,** but you **don't have to read** a magazine while you are waiting.

Questions

1. What is the meaning of *must* and *have to* in sentences 1 and 3?

2. Is the meaning of *must not* in sentence 2 the same as the meaning of *don't have to* in sentence 3? How is the grammar different in these two sentences?

Explanation—*Must/Have To* in Negative Sentences

1. Negative sentences with *must* and *have to*

   a. **RULE:** Add the word *not* after the auxiliary.

      You *must not (mustn't*) enter* the building through that door.
      You *must not (mustn't*) smoke* in the hospital.

   Follow this pattern for negative sentences using *must:*

subject	auxiliary	*not*	verb (simple form)	
You	must	not	enter	the building through that door.
You	must	not	smoke	in the hospital.

   b. To make a negative sentence with *have to,* add *not* after the auxiliary *do.*

      You *do not (don't*) have to read* a magazine while you are waiting.
      She *does not (doesn't*) have to see* the doctor for her cold.
      I *did not (didn't*) have to go* to the hospital for my foot injury.

   ---
   *Contractions are often used in conversation. They are not usually used in formal writing.

If the sentence is in the future, use the auxiliary *will* and not the auxiliary *do*.

They *will not (won't*) have to return* to the doctor until the next checkup appointment.

Follow this pattern for negative sentences using *have to*:

subject	auxiliary	*not*	*have to* + verb	
You	do	not	have to read	a magazine.
She	does	not	have to see	the doctor.
I	did	not	have to go	to the hospital.
They	will	not	have to return	to the doctor.

NOTE: Do not use *have got to* in negative statements.

2. *Must not* has a strong meaning. It says that something is prohibited or not allowed. It involves a requirement, and there is no choice in this situation.

  You *must not use* a door that has a Do Not Enter sign. (This is a requirement.)

  You *must not smoke* in a hospital. (This is a rule or a law. Smoking is not allowed.)

3. The negative forms of *have to* are not as strong. They indicate that something is not necessary, and that there is a choice.

  You *don't have to read* a magazine in the waiting room. (This is your choice. You can read a magazine if you like, but it is not necessary.)

  You *don't have to buy* that brand of medicine. (This is your choice. You can buy another brand if you like.)

Activity 4

A patient is at a doctor's office for a medical test right now. Circle the word or expression in parentheses that best fits the situation.

Receptionist: First, you (must/must not) sign this form. It gives us permission to perform this procedure.

Patient: (I do have to/Do I have to) sign it right now?

Receptionist: Yes, it is required. You (have to/don't have to) sign it before we do anything else. Thank you. Now please go with the nurse into Room 3.

---

*Contractions are often used in conversation. They are not usually used in formal writing.

Nurse: You (must/don't have to) wear this gown, so please put it on immediately.

Patient: I'd like to keep my watch on. Is that okay?

Nurse: Yes, that's fine. You (must not/do not have to) remove all of your jewelry. Also, during the procedure it's important not to move. You (must not/must) keep your arms still and at your sides at all times. You (don't have to/must not) move them up and down or away from your body.

Patient: I'm getting a little nervous. I hope I (have to/don't have to) lie still like that for a very long time.

Nurse: No. It's a short procedure. If you are nervous, or if it feels uncomfortable, you might want to squeeze this little rubber ball. You (must not/don't have to) use it, but you can if you like.

Activity 5

Fill in each space with one of the following: must, have to, must not, *or* doesn't/don't have to.

1. Janet: I bought some strong medicine for my back pain today.

    Barbara: You _____ keep it where your young children can't find it. It doesn't have a childproof safety cap. You _____ leave it out or within their reach.

2. Store clerk: Here's some medicine with a childproof safety cap.

    Customer: I _____ get that one. I don't have any children at home.

    Store clerk: You _____ buy it that way. It's the only kind we carry.

3. The law requires car seats for all children under five years of age in this state. It also requires everyone in the vehicle to wear seat belts. This means:

    a. Young children _____ ride in a car seat at all times in this state.

b. A young child _____ ride in a car without a car seat in this state.

c. An older child _____ wear seat belts.

d. An adult _____ drive or be in the vehicle without a seat belt.

4. The school district requires all children to have a physical checkup and all their vaccinations before they enter school at the beginning of the year.

a. Cindy's child had a check up but is not up-to-date with her shots. Her child _____ gets some vaccinations before she enters school this year.

b. Elaine's child has had all his shots but has not had a checkup in two years. Her child _____ get any shots but he _____ go for a checkup.

c. Glen's son just had a physical two weeks ago and is now up-to-date with his vaccinations. His son _____ get any shots or see the doctor again now.

Activity 6

A. *Look at the following labels on different medications and write two sentences of instructions of what to do or not to do. One sentence should be negative and one should be positive, and each sentence must include one of the following: must, have to, must not, or don't have to. The first one has been done as an example.*

1. You have to wait at least four hours before you take more tablets.

    You must be careful about how many tablets you take in 24 hours.

    You don't have to take two tablets each time.

    You must not take more than 6 tablets in 24 hours.

> ℞ Take one or two tablets every 4 to 6 hours. Do not take more than 6 tablets in 24 hours.

2. _____

    _____

    _____

    _____

    _____

    _____

> 👁 Can cause drowsiness. Alcohol will increase that effect. Use care when operating a car or machine with this medicine.

3. _____

   _____

   _____

   _____

   _____

> Be sure to drink water with this medication. It may be taken with food or without.

> **Rx** For external use only. Avoid getting this medication in eyes or mouth.

4. _____

   _____

   _____

   _____

   _____

5. _____

   _____

   _____

   _____

   _____

> **Rx** Use once or twice a day when needed for rash. Use only when rash is present.

B. *Read each of the following situations and write questions and answers about what the person or people (a) must, (b) must not, (c) has/have got to, (d) has/have to, or (e) don't/doesn't have to do in each case. The first one has been done as an example.*

1. A woman is walking away from a parked car and into the direction of a store. You can see a small child in a car seat in the car.

   Question: What does this woman have to do in this situation?

   Answer: She must (has to/has got to) take the child with her.

   Question: Does she have to take the child out of the car?

   Answer: Yes, she must not leave the child alone in the car.

   Question: Does she have to do her shopping right now?

   Answer: Yes, she has got to shop now, but she must not leave the

   child alone.

   She must not go shopping now if she can't take the child with her.

2. A woman and child are standing in front of a door that is labeled "restrooms." There is a sign on the door that says, "Closed for cleaning. Please use restrooms at other end of the mall."

   _____

   _____

   _____

   _____

3. Two cars are on the side of the road and the drivers are looking at the front bumper of one and the back bumper of the other. It is clear they just had a "fender bender" accident. One man is holding his neck.

_____

_____

_____

_____

_____

4. A customer is standing in a store between a prescription counter and an aisle of over-the-counter medication. The prescription counter has a sign that says, "Prescriptions filled." The customer is confused.

_____

_____

_____

_____

5. A baby or small child is sitting on the floor holding a box that says "Floor cleaner—Warning: poison." It's clear that she has eaten some of it. A teenager is standing near a telephone.

_____

_____

_____

_____

6. Two people are leaving a party. The host is standing at the door with a drink in his hand. The people leaving are walking toward a car.

_____

_____

_____

_____

Possibility: Less Certain

May/Might/Could

Presentation 1

Questions

1. What is the meaning of the three modals in bold in sentences 2 and 3?

2. Are these words strong or weak in meaning?

¹Cindy wants to follow a healthier lifestyle. ²She **could join** a fitness club, or she **might try** walking and hiking in the park near her house. ³She also **may be** ready to start a new diet and change her eating habits.

Explanation—Using *May/Might/Could* for Possibility

1. The modals *could, may,* and *might* indicate possibility. We use these modals when we are not sure about a situation and want to give the meaning of *perhaps* or *maybe*.

    She *could join* a fitness club. She *might try* walking and hiking.

    She *may be* ready to start a new diet.

    NOTE: Do not confuse the word *maybe* (one word) with *may be* (two words).

    may + be = modal auxiliary + verb: She *may be* ready to start a new diet.

Maybe is not a verb. It is an adverb and is often at the beginning of a sentence.

Maybe she is ready to start a new diet.

2.   These three modals follow the grammar rules for all modals. (See page 91.)

She *could join* a fitness club. They *may be* ready to start a new diet.

3.   **Negative sentences**

RULE: Add the word *not* after the auxiliary.

She *might not try* walking and hiking. They *may not be* ready to start a new diet.

Follow this pattern for negative sentences using *may* and *might:*

subject	auxiliary	not	verb (simple form)	
She	might	not	try	walking and hiking.
They	may	not	be	ready to start a new diet.

NOTE: We do not use *could* in negative sentences for this meaning. *Could not* indicates something is impossible or almost impossible. It is stronger than *may not* and *might not* when negative.

My friend says she lost 20 pounds in two weeks on her diet. That *couldn't be* true. (It seems impossible.)

4.   **Questions**

For this meaning, we usually use only the word *could* for questions.

a.   **Yes/no questions**

RULE: Place the auxiliary to the left of the subject of the sentence.

Could we *try* hiking in the park? *Could* they *be* ready to start a new diet? *Could* she *fail* on that diet?

Follow this pattern for yes/no questions using *could:*

auxiliary	subject	verb (simple form)	
Could	we	try	hiking in the park?
Could	they	be	ready to start a new diet?
Could	she	fail	on that diet?

b. **Question word questions**

Place the question word and the auxiliary to the left of the subject.

How could she *fail* on that diet? *Why could* we *lose* our membership at the gym? *Where could* they *find* a cheaper fitness club?

Follow this pattern for question word questions using *could:*

question word	auxiliary	subject	verb (simple form)	
How	could	she	fail	on that diet?
Why	could	we	lose	our membership at the gym?
Where	could	they	find	a cheaper fitness club?

5. We use *could, may,* and *might* to indicate possibility in both present and future situations.

   She *may be* ready to start a new diet. She *might start* it tomorrow.

   They *could join* a fitness club. They *may visit* the one near school next week.

Practice

Activity 1

Match each statement in the column on the left with the possibility from the column on the right.

_____ 1. I'm thinking of joining the new fitness club near school.

_____ 2. Where is John and why isn't he eating lunch with us?

a. He might be on a diet.

b. Could I join that group? I need to relax more.

_____ 3. How will you change your diet?

c. I might eat less meat. I might even become a vegetarian.

_____ 4. What are some natural remedies for laryngitis?

d. Hot tea and honey could help.

_____ 5. Why didn't he eat the birthday cake?

e. I may visit it tonight and try out some of the machines.

_____ 6. My friend and I joined a yoga group at school.

f. He could be eating a salad in his office.

Activity 2

Find six mistakes in the following conversation.

Glenn: Why is Sandy absent from school today?

Susan: She may is at the Health Clinic. She has been sick for the past
            few days.

Glenn: What's the problem? She was fine last week.

Susan: She isn't sure. It maybe a bad cold, or she might to have a
            sinus infection.

Glenn: Will she be able to come with us on the field trip tomorrow
            morning?

Susan: She no might make it to that. We don't want anyone with an
            infirmity on the trip.

Glenn: Do you think her illness could it be communicable?

Susan: Yes, it's possible. We'll know more when she comes back from
            the clinic. May be the practitioner there will prescribe some
            medicine for her.

Activity 3

A. Ben, Debbie, Rob, and Nick have
    just joined a fitness club, and they
    are deciding what they will do there.
    At the right you will find a flyer from
    the club that shows some of the
    activities available to choose from.

1. Read the information about each
    person's situation on the next page.
2. Decide what each person may,
    might, or could do based on the flyer
    and the information about the per-
    son. Write two or three sentences
    about the different possibilities for
    each person, using the modals may,
    might, *and* could.

Ben: He loves to swim but doesn't like to use machines. He wants to learn to play racquetball. He is willing to take some classes. He can only go in the evenings.

Debbie: She loves yoga and also wants to try some new kinds of classes. She has never used any exercise machines and would like to learn more about them.

Rob: He doesn't know how to swim, but he loves to play racquetball. He needs to lose some weight, so he is looking forward to using some machines.

Nick: He has done some weight lifting and used some machines, but he wants to learn more about them.

EXAMPLE:

Nick: He might go to the weight room. **OR** He could work with a personal trainer. **OR** He may want to ask for information.

B. *What kinds of activities do you think you might try at a fitness club? Imagine you are visiting the same club described in the flyer. Write two or three sentences about different possibilities of things for you to try there, using* may, might, *or* could *in your answers.*

_____

_____

_____

_____

_____

_____

_____

_____

_____

_____

_____

Presentation 2

Using *May, Might*, and *Could* with Progressive Verbs

[1]Andrea is young, but she **might be harming** her future health with some of her present lifestyle choices. [2]She **could be making** plans for some changes in order to stay in better shape. [3]In the future she **may be eating** more healthy food or spending more time at the gym.

Questions

1. What ending is on the verbs in bold in these sentences? What auxiliaries are before these verbs?

2. What is the time in sentences 1 and 2? What is the time in sentence 3?

3. How can you make these sentences negative? How can you make them questions?

Explanation—Possibility and the Progressive

1. We can also use these modals for something that is possibly happening now or in the future by making them progressive. In these cases follow this pattern: modal + be + verb + -*ing*

    Andrea *might be harming* her future health. We *could be making* plans for some changes. In the future they *may be eating* more healthy food.

2. **Negative sentences**

    RULE: Add the word *not* after the *first* auxiliary.

    Andrea *might not be harming* her future health with her present lifestyle.

    We *may not be joining* a health club in the near future.

    Follow this pattern for negative sentences using *may* and *might* and the progressive:

subject	auxiliary	not	auxiliary *(be)*	verb + -*ing*	
Andrea	might	not	be	harming	her future health.
We	may	not	be	joining	a health club.

    NOTE: We do not use *could* in negative sentences in the progressive for this meaning.

3. **Questions**

    We don't usually use *may, might,* and *could* for questions about future possibilities. We use *could* for questions about present possibilities using the progressive.

a. **Yes/no questions**

RULE: Move the *first* auxiliary to the left of the subject of the sentence.

Could she *be harming* her future health? *Could* he *be changing* his diet to become a vegetarian?

Follow this pattern for yes/no questions using *could:*

auxiliary	subject	auxiliary *(be)*	verb + *-ing*	
Could	she	be	harming	her future health?
Could	he	be	changing	his diet to become a vegetarian?

b. **Question word questions**

Place the question word and the first auxiliary to the left of the subject.

Where could she *be taking* a yoga class? *How could* you *be failing* on your new diet?

Follow this pattern for question word questions using *could:*

Question word	auxiliary	subject	auxiliary *(be)*	verb + *-ing*	
Where	could	she	be	taking	a yoga class?
How	could	you	be	failing	on your new diet?

Activity 4

Fill in the spaces of the story using one of the verbs below and the modal in parentheses. Your answers should all be in the progressive. Use each verb only once.

> prepare   store   make   sanitize   start   try   grow   take

1. My mother is in the kitchen taking out chicken, carrots, and onions.

   She (could) _____ some chicken soup for her cold.

2. Adam is cutting a small piece off an aloe plant.

   He (might) _____ it to put on the cut on his finger.

3. Jill is boiling some water and getting honey and tea ready.

   She (may) _____ some medicinal tea for her sore throat.

4. Megan is sitting in the corner of the room with her eyes closed.

   She (might) _____ to meditate to relieve some stress.

5. Greg is putting some dried herbs in bottles.

   He (could) _____ them to use when he is sick.

6. Cindy is asking her boss for a 15-minute break every morning at 10:00 a.m.

   She (may) _____ to schedule a daily relaxation break at work.

7. Jack is planting some organic herbs in his garden.

   He (might) _____ them for medicinal purposes.

8. Cheri is putting all of her storage bottles in boiling water.

   She (may) _____ them before she stores her herbs.

Activity 5

A. *Rewrite each sentence. Add the idea of "maybe" or "perhaps" by adding* may, could, *or* might, *keeping the sentence in the progressive. You should use each of the modals twice.*

   EXAMPLE: He is staying home to relax today.

   He may be staying home to relax today. **OR** He might be staying home
   to relax today. **OR** He could be staying home to relax today.

1. He is going to the gym after work tomorrow.

   _____

2. I am starting a new diet today.

   _____

3. My friends are enrolling in a new Pilates class tonight.

   _____

4. Jack is running a 10K race next month and a marathon in three months.

   _____

5. My gym is buying new exercise bikes to replace the old ones.

   _____

6. Some people are having a problem using the new equipment at the gym.

   _____

B. *Rewrite the sentences you wrote above using* may *and* might *in the negative.*

Activity 6

Work in small groups for this activity.

A. Look at the following photographs. Discuss what you think could, may, or might *be happening in these pictures. Think about the following questions and discuss your ideas with the others in your group.*

Who are the people in these pictures?   Where are they?

Why are they there?   What are they doing?

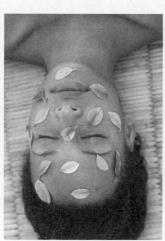

B. *Choose one picture and create a short story or explanation about what you think is taking place. Your story should be at least five or six sentences. Be sure to use the modals from this lesson (can/might/could) in your sentences and use some of the verbs in the progressive. Share your story with the rest of the class.*

_____

_____

_____

_____

_____

_____

_____

_____

_____

_____

_____

Probability and Expectation: More Certain

Must/Should/Ought To

Presentation 1

Questions

1. What is the meaning of *must* in these sentences?

2. What is the time in these sentences?

3. How can you make these sentences negative?

[1]Alyssa is home from work today. [2]She **must be** sick. [3]She has a thermometer in her mouth, so she **must be** taking her temperature. [4]She **must be** upset because she is missing an important meeting at work.

Explanation—*Must* for Conclusions/Probability

1. You have already learned about using the modal *must* for necessity or obligation. Sometimes we use *must* to make a conclusion about people or situations based on information we already know about them.

   We see someone in bed with a thermometer, so we can make the following conclusions:

   She *must be* sick. She *must feel* too sick to go to work.

2. In Lesson 17 you learned about words that show possibility *(could/might/may)*. In some cases you might use these words for conclusions, but they are not as strong as *must* for this meaning. A conclusion with *must* is stronger than a possibility.

   25%   50%   90–95%

   not sure/possibly = might/could/may—   more sure/probably = must—

She is not answering her telephone. She *could/may/might be* out. (possibility—She might also be taking a shower or sleeping.)

She is in bed and has a thermometer in her mouth. She *must be* feeling sick. (probably—other situations are not likely)

She is missing an important meeting at work today. She *must* be upset.

3. The modal *must* follows the grammar rules for all modals. (See page 91.)

   RULE: Add the word *not* after the auxiliary.

   She *must be* sick. She *must feel* too sick to go to work.

4. Negative sentences with *must* as a conclusion

   You *must not be* sick. She *must not feel* too sick to go to work.

Follow this pattern for negative sentences using *must:*

subject	auxiliary	not	verb (simple form)	
You	must	not	be	sick.
She	must	not	feel	too sick to go to work.

NOTE: Do not use the contraction *(mustn't)* in a negative conclusion using *must.*

5. We can also use *must* for a conclusion about something happening right now by using the progressive. In this case we use the following pattern:

   must + be + verb + *-ing*

   She *must be taking* her temperature. You *must be staying* home from work today.

   He *must not be attending* his classes today.

Practice

Activity 1

A. *Fill in each blank below with a conclusion using the modal* must *and the verb in parentheses. Make the sentence negative where indicated.*

   EXAMPLE:

   Who is that man sitting in the waiting room?

   I've never seen him before. He (be) _____ a new patient.

   He <u>must be</u> a new patient.

1. Why does that person wear a white uniform every day?

    He (work) _____ in the health clinic across the street.

2. Why is that man holding an icepack to his head?

   He (have) _____ an injury there.

3. Why is the pharmacy clerk ignoring the people waiting at the door to get in?

   It (be—negative) _____ time to open for business yet.

4. I work in the laboratory of that hospital.

   You (know) _____ my friend Joe. He works there too.

5. Why is the receptionist telling that man the doctor cannot see him today?

   He (have—negative) _____ an appointment for today.

6. How does she keep in such good health?

   She (eat) _____ healthy food and exercises a lot.

7. Where can I buy that strong medicine for my headache?

   It (be) _____ available at the large pharmacy downtown.

B. *Fill in each blank below with a conclusion using the modal* must *and a progressive form of the verb in parentheses.*

   EXAMPLE:

   Q: Why are those people in line for the cashier?

   A: They (wait) <u>must be waiting</u> to pay for their prescriptions.

   1. Why is Susan spending so much time exercising and running?

      She (train) _____ for her next marathon. She loves to run those.

   2. People have been calling in sick all week.

      Many people (catch) _____ Joe's bad cold.

   3. Why is Bill closing his eyes and taking deep breaths?

      He (try) _____ to relax.

   4. Why is that patient back to see the doctor for the second time this week?

      Her health (improve—negative) _____ fast enough.

   5. Why is that ambulance stopping in front of your neighbor's house?

      The paramedics (respond) _____ to an emergency there.

   6. Where do you think the receptionist is? There is nobody at the desk right now.

      She said she had a question for the nurse. She (talk) _____ to her.

7. Can you hear that little boy crying at the nurse's clinic?

He (get) _____ a shot. That's the room for vaccinations.

Activity 2

Each sentence below contains the modal must. *In some cases the* must *means obligation or necessity, and in other sentences it is a conclusion showing a strong possibility. Write O for obligation or necessity and C for conclusion or probability.*

_____ 1. You must have a prescription to buy certain kinds of medicine.

_____ 2. You must make an appointment to see a doctor at that clinic.

_____ 3. He must be sleeping because he has a bad headache and is not answering the telephone.

_____ 4. That young boy with the red hair and blue eyes must be Jill's son.

_____ 5. You must drink a full glass of water with that medicine.

_____ 6. Betty must be tired after all that exercising she did at the gym today.

_____ 7. I must get to the pharmacy to pick up my medicine before it closes at 6:00 p.m.

_____ 8. Rogerio must like to swim because I see him at the pool almost every day.

_____ 9. You must be very happy about finishing your nursing program this semester.

_____ 10. All patients must make future appointments at the receptionist's desk.

Activity 3

Read each numbered statement below. Then write a sentence that expresses a conclusion about something that is probably true based on the information in the sentence. Use the modal must *and the words in parentheses in each answer. Use the* must + be + verb + -ing *pattern if possible in some of your answers.*

EXAMPLE:

Jane always keeps in shape by swimming and lifting weights.
(a membership at the gym)

Jane must have a membership at the gym. **OR** *Jane must use her*

membership at the gym often.

1. Janet is in the waiting room of the dentist's office holding the side of her mouth. (a toothache)

_____

2. The dentist is showing Janet an x-ray of her tooth. (a cavity in that tooth)

_____

3. Two patients have just arrived at the doctor's office and are at the receptionist now. (check in)

_____

4. Those people are reading a directory of the clinic at the entrance. (look for the doctor's office)

_____

5. That man in the white uniform leaves the clinic every day at 5 p.m. (work there)

_____

6. The woman in the elevator is wearing a cast on her leg. (a broken leg)

_____

7. Those two people are communicating in sign language. (hearing impaired)

_____

8. Bob is looking at his calendar and talking to the receptionist. (make a new appointment)

_____

9. The label on the medicine bottle says it expired 6 months ago. (too old to use)

_____

Presentation 2

Using *Should* and *Ought To* for Expectations

Patient: I have a 3:00 p.m. appointment with the doctor, and it's now 3:30. Is there a problem?

Receptionist: An emergency at the hospital kept her there a long time. She called and said she was trying to leave as soon as possible. She **ought to be** on her way. She **should be arriving** here any minute.

Questions

1. What is the meaning of *should* and *ought to* in these sentences?

2. What is the time in the last two sentences?

3. How can you make the last sentence a question?

Explanation—Expectations—*Should* and *Ought To*

1. Sometimes we can have an expectation of something based on information we already know. It could be something about a present situation or more often about something we expect for the future. In these cases we use the expression *ought to* or the modal *should* to express that expectation. This expectation is not as strong as a conclusion with *must*.

    NOTE: *Ought to* is considered more formal than *should*.

    a. She *should be/ought to be* on her way.

     She called and said she was trying to leave as soon as possible. Therefore, I can expect or make a conclusion that if the situation did not change, she is probably on her way to the office.

    b. She *must be* on her way.

     She called and said that she was getting into her car at that moment and would get to the office as fast as she could. I can make a stronger conclusion that she is on her way.

2. *Should* and *ought to* follow the same grammar rules discussed in Lesson 15. (See page 99.)

3. **Negative sentences**

    RULE: Add the word *not* after the auxiliary.

     Your wait *should not (shouldn't*) be* much longer. The drive here *should not take* too long.

     She *should not (shouldn't*) be taking* this long to get here.

    Follow this pattern for negative sentences using *should*:

subject	auxiliary	not	verb (simple form)	
Your wait	should	not	be	much longer.
The drive here	should	not	take	too long.

subject	auxiliary	not	auxiliary *(be)*	verb + *-ing*	
She	should	not	be	taking	this long to get here.

    NOTE: We do not usually use *ought to* in negative sentences.

4. **Questions**

    RULE: Place the auxiliary to the left of the subject of the sentence.

     Should the doctor *be* here soon?

    Yes/no questions:

auxiliary	subject	verb (simple form)	
Should	the doctor	be	here soon?

---

*Contractions are often used in conversation. They are not usually used in formal writing.

RULE: Place the auxiliary after the question word and before the subject of the sentence.

When *should* the doctor *be* here?

Wh- questions:

question word	auxiliary	subject	verb (simple form)	
When	should	the doctor	be	here?

Activity 4

A. *Each numbered item in the list below contains a question and an answer. Change each answer from a definite statement to an expectation using* ought to *or* should. *If the sentence is negative, make your expectation negative as well.*

EXAMPLE:

Q: Where is the doctor?   A: She is on her way.

She should be on her way. **OR** She ought to be on her way.

1. Where can I buy this medicine at a better price?
    You find it cheaper at the discount pharmacy across the street.

    _____

2. Doctor, how long will it take for my condition to improve?
    It takes about two or three days with this medication.

    _____

3. Does it hurt to apply that poultice to my arm?
    It doesn't hurt at all.

    _____

4. Are these exercise machines easy to use?
    Most of them are not difficult to use at all.

    _____

5. Will my teeth cleaning take more than half an hour?
    No, it doesn't take longer than that.

    _____

6. How long does it take for this herbal tea to help my sore throat?
    It helps the soreness after about two or three cups.

    _____

B. *Change each answer from a definite statement to an expectation using* ought to *or* should *and the progressive of the verb. Make the sentence negative (using* should*) where indicated in parentheses as well.*

EXAMPLE:

Will I see the doctor soon? The nurse is getting ready to call you in.

The nurse should/ought to be getting ready to call you in.

1. Nurse, where is the doctor? I've been waiting in this exam room for over half an hour.
    He is coming in just a few minutes.

    _____

2. Why is the cut on my arm still infected?
    I don't know. It is healing so slowly. (negative)

    _____

3. Will I get the results of my x-rays today?
    Yes, the technician is developing them now.

    _____

4. I think the herbal remedy you gave me is keeping me up at night.
    That is stopping you from sleeping. (negative)

    _____

5. When will Jack return from the gym?
    It's 5:00 p.m. He is finishing his workout soon.

    _____

 Activity 5

Find six mistakes in the following conversation and correct them.

Receptionist: Hello. This is Doctor Marshall's office calling. Is Marcia there? She is late for her 3:00 p.m. appointment with the doctor.

Sister: She left about 15 minutes ago, so she ought be there by now.

Receptionist: Well, she is very late and we cannot wait much longer.

Sister: She should be arrive any minute. I don't know why she isn't there yet. She must is caught in traffic. Her cell phone shoulds be on. I'll try calling her.

Receptionist: If she is stuck in traffic, she ought to calling us to let us know.

Sister: I should am able to call you back after I speak to her.

Activity 6

Work with a partner for this exercise. Below you will see three photographs. Look at each photo and write some conclusions and expectations about what you think is probably happening or will probably happen. Be sure to write complete sentences using must *in your conclusions and* should *or* ought to *in your expectations. Try to use the progressive in some of your sentences as well. The questions below the photographs can help you think about what to write.*

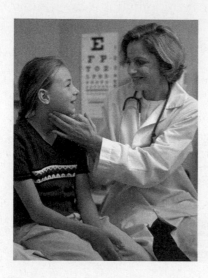

Questions

1. Who are these people?
2. Where are they?
3. Why are they there?
4. What are they doing?
5. What are they saying?

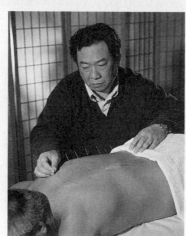

Past Advisability

Should/Ought To/ Could/Might

Presentation

Questions

1. Look at the bold words in sentence 3. How many auxiliaries do you see with the verbs? What form of the verb follows these auxiliaries?

2. What is the time in sentences 2 and 3?

3. What is the meaning of each of the modals in bold in sentences 2 and 3?

[1]John has been sick for several days, but today is the first day he is staying home. [2]He **should have stayed** home before this and **should not have gone** to work. [3]He **could have tried** to take some natural remedies, or he **might have called** the doctor for advice. [4]However, he did not do any of these things, and now he feels much worse than before.

Explanation—Past Advisability

1. *Should have, ought to have, could have,* and *might have* express the idea that something was advisable or a good idea in the past, but it was not done. In addition, these forms indicate that someone is sorry or regrets that no action was taken. It may indicate that someone is angry or upset about something *not* said or done.

   He *should have stayed* home before this. It was a good idea to stay home, but he didn't do it. Now he is very sick. He is sorry he did not stay home.

He *could have tried* some natural remedies. Taking natural remedies was a good idea, but he did not do that.

She *should have told* him about her illness. She didn't tell him about her illness and now he is sick, too. He is upset about that.

2. When we use these modals or the expression *ought to* in the past, we follow several grammar rules you have already studied. The modals *should, could,* and *have* and the expression *ought to* are followed by the simple form of the auxiliary *have,* and the auxiliary *have* is followed by the past participle of the verb.

> She/He *should have stayed* home before this. She/He *could have tried* some natural remedies.

> I *ought to have tried* some natural remedies. They *might have called* the doctor for some advice.

NOTE: In conversation, you may hear the following short forms. You should never write these forms, but you will hear native speakers use them in conversation.

should have	You will hear *shoulda.*
could have	You will hear *coulda.*

In addition, do not write *could of* or *should of* for these forms.

3. **Negative sentences**

For past advisability we use only *should* in negative sentences.

RULE: Add the word *not* after the *first* auxiliary.

> She *should not (shouldn't*) have gone* to work. You *should not (shouldn't*) have tried* to prepare that home remedy by yourself.

Follow this pattern for negative sentences using *should* for past advisability:

subject	auxiliary	not	auxiliary *(have)*	verb (past participle)	
She	should	not	have	gone	to work.
You	should	not	have	tried	to prepare . . .

4. **Questions**

Usually we use only *should* in questions about past advisability.

a. **Yes/no questions**

RULE: Place the *first* auxiliary to the left of the subject of the sentence.

> *Should* she *have gone* to a doctor? *Should* I *have taken* some medicine for the pain?

---

*Contractions are often used in conversation. They are not usually used in formal writing.

Follow this pattern for yes/no questions using *should* for past advisability:

auxiliary	subject	auxiliary *(have)*	verb (past participle)	
Should	she	have	gone	to a doctor?
Should	I	have	taken	some medicine for the pain?

b. **Question word questions**

RULE: Place the question word and the first auxiliary to the left of the subject.

Why should she *have gone* to a doctor? *When should* I *have taken* the medicine?

Follow this pattern for question word questions using *should* for past advisability:

question word	auxiliary	subject	auxiliary *(have)*	verb (past participle)	
Why	should	she	have	gone	to a doctor?
When	should	I	have	taken	the medicine?

Practice

Activity 1

Read each statement and then write T *for true or* F *for false for each sentence that follows. The first one has been done as an example.*

1. He ought to have asked the nurse practitioner about the side effects of that medicine.

   __F__ He asked the nurse practitioner about the side effects.

2. You should have gone to sleep early last night because of your bad cold.

   _____ You went to sleep early last night.

3. You might have bought a different medicine because yours was not helping you.

   _____ You tried only one kind of cough medicine.

4. She should not have taken her sister's medicine before she talked to a doctor.

   _____ She took her sister's medicine, but she did not talk to a doctor about it.

5. They could have signed up for the medical insurance at their job.

   _____ They did not take the medical insurance their job offered.

6. We could have tried the home remedy you gave us, but we did not have any honey.

   _____ We did not try the home remedy.

7. He should not have exercised so much with his bad back.

   _____ He exercised very little because of his back problem.

8. She was accepted to medical school, so she could have become a doctor.

   _____ She went to medical school, and she became a doctor.

Activity 2 *(Review transitions: Unit Three, pages 77–85.)*

Find two or three mistakes in each of the following situations and show how to correct them. You should find a total of eight mistakes.

1. Bob entered his first marathon last week. However, he did not achieve his goal because he could not finish the race. He should has trained harder; in addition, he should have not quit the race. He stopped only two miles from the finish line.

2. One child came to school with a communicable illness; moreover, now several children in that class are sick. The parents of that child could taken him to the doctor but they did not. Instead, they sent him to school with a fever. They should not have send the child to school. They coulda at least called the doctor to ask for advice.

3. Linda has had a chronic problem with pain in her wrist for a long time. Several people have given her advice about it, but she has refused to listen to anyone.

   • Her best friend told her about her success with acupuncture. Linda might of gotten the information about her friend's acupuncturist.

   • Her brother told her to see his chiropractor. Linda could have tryed to see him.

   • Her aunt gave her instructions for an herbal remedy for the pain. Linda should not laughed at that suggestion.

Activity 3

Complete each sentence in the following conversations to express regret or say something about what was advisable in the past. Use the modal or expression given in parentheses and one of the verbs listed below. Use each verb only once. The first one has been done as an example.

stop	think	warn	call	take	shop

1. Gary: I'm sorry I didn't listen to you about going to a holistic doctor.

   Ilene: You (should) <u>should have taken</u> my advice. That doctor has always helped me with my problems.

2. Garrett: I was trying to watch my diet and eat healthy foods last month, but I was not successful.

   Kayla: You (ought to) _____ at the new health food store for your groceries. They have many different kinds of organic vegetables.

3. Sam: The doctor prescribed some medicine, but I only took it for two days.

   Lois: The label on the bottle says to take all of it. You (should—negative) _____ taking it.

4. Jean: I knew that exercise machine would not be good for your back.

   Ellie: You (might) _____ me about it. I used it for half an hour yesterday, and now I am in pain.

5. Patient: I'm sorry I am so late for my appointment with the doctor.

   Receptionist: You (could) _____ to tell us you were running late.

6. Seth: The neighbors are sorry they used chemicals on the vegetables in their garden.

   Scot: I know. They (should) _____ about the ecosystem and their health when they did that.

Activity 4   *(Review transitions: Unit Three, pages 77–85.)*

For each of the following situations, write a response about something that was advisable or a good idea in the past but was not done. Write a complete sentence using the words in parentheses and adding words of your own as well.

EXAMPLE: Jill had a bad cold yesterday, but she went to work anyway.

(should stay home) *Jill should have stayed home from work yesterday.*

(should—negative—go) *Jill should not have gone to work yesterday.*

1. Cindy missed the 3:00 pm yoga class; therefore, she went home.

   (could stay for another class) _____

   _____

   (ought to wait for the next class) _____

   _____

   (should leave so quickly—negative) _____

   _____

2. Jim went to his dentist's office at noon without an appointment; as a result, he could not see her.

   (should call before) _____

   _____

   (could try make an appointment) _____

   _____

   (should just walk in—negative) _____

   _____

3. Bill's prescription medicine was very expensive, but he bought it.

   (might buy generic brand) _____

   _____

   (could shop around pharmacies) _____

   _____

4. The babysitter bought the wrong kind of medicine for the child.

(should get the childproof bottle)

_____

_____

(ought to purchase syrup not pills)

_____

_____

(might pick orange-flavored medicine)

_____

_____

(should choose adult kind—negative)

_____

_____

Activity 5   *(Review transitions: Unit Three, pages 77–85.)*

Read each of the step-by-step instructions below. Then, read how someone tried to follow each set of instructions but was unsuccessful or did something wrong. Write two or three sentences about what the person should have, ought to have, might have, or could have done to be successful. Then, write a negative sentence using should *in the past as well.*

EXAMPLE:

Instructions: Walking program to exercise and reduce stress

Step 1: stretch and warm up—10 to 15 minutes
a. stretch legs, feet, and toes
b. do knee bends
c. warm up by walking slowly

Step 2: fast walking—45 to 50 minutes
a. increase speed as you walk
b. breathe correctly and check heart rate

Olga had less than an hour to do her exercise; as a result, she did not warm up. She had leg pains when she finished her walk.

She should have (ought to have) warmed up and walked for less time.

She could have (might have) waited for another time to do her exercise.

She should not have skipped her warm up.

Instructions: Relaxing with a meditative technique

Step 1: be comfortable

a. find a comfortable place to sit

b. sit in a comfortable position

c. wear comfortable clothing

Step 2: have a passive attitude and clear mind

a. practice deep breathing

b. close eyes and concentrate

Robert tried to relax with this technique in his office at work wearing a suit and tie. His phone rang several times, and two people knocked on his office door.

_____

_____

_____

_____

Instructions for using a poultice or plaster

Step 1: preparing the herb

a. take dried or powdered herb

   for poultice: use "cool" herb like comfrey or flax seed

   for plaster: use any herb including hot mustard or cayenne pepper

b. mix herb with hot water

c. make a paste with the water and flour or oatmeal

Step 2: application

a. poultice: put the paste directly on the skin

   hold the paste on the skin with a warm cloth or bandage

b. plaster: put paste in a cloth, such as cheesecloth, and apply the cloth to the skin

Gary wanted to make a poultice. He used some pepper as his herb, and he put the paste on his skin. When he did this, his skin became red and felt burning.

_____

_____

_____

_____

Instructions for preparing homemade special syrup for colds and cough

Step 1: preparing onions

a.   slice two or three onions

b.   put onions in a liter of water and boil them

Step 2: sweetening the mixture

a.   make sure the water is still boiling

b.   add sugar or honey to boiling water (sweeten to taste)

c.   cool the mixture to form syrup

Jackie did not have a lot of time; therefore, she did not boil the onions in the water. She cooked the onions for a few minutes. Then, she added some sugar. The sugar did not dissolve; furthermore, the mixture did not become syrup.

_____

_____

_____

_____

Past Possibility and Probability

Might/Could/May/Must/Had To

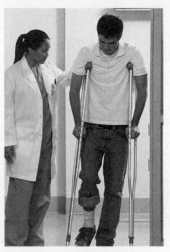

Presentation

Questions

1. Look at all the bold words in these sentences. How many auxiliaries do you see with the verbs? What form of the verb follows these auxiliaries?

2. What is the time in all of these sentences?

3. What is the meaning of each of the modals? Which of the modals in these sentences is the strongest one?

[1]Armando **must have broken** his ankle. [2]He **could have had** an accident at school. [3]He **may have been** in a car accident. [4]He **might have hurt** himself while playing sports.

Explanation—Past Possibility and Probability

1. *Might have, may have, could have, had to have,* and *must have* are all used to express a possibility or a guess about something that happened in the past. However, they do not all indicate the same degree of certainty.

| might have | may have | could have | had to have | must have |

A. He *must have/had to have broken* his ankle. In this case we see the person in a cast and on crutches; therefore, we can make a strong conclusion and be fairly certain that this person broke his ankle.

B. He *could have had* an accident at school. He *may have been* in a car accident. He *might have hurt* himself while playing sports.

In these examples, we are making more of a guess. These are all possibilities, but we are not very sure which one really happened.

2. When we use these modals/expressions in the past, we follow several grammar rules you have already studied. The modals *might, may, could,* and *must* and the expression *had to* (past of *have to*) are followed by the simple form of the auxiliary *have,* and the auxiliary *have* is followed by the past participle of the verb.

    He *must have/had to have broken* his ankle. They *might have hurt* themselves during the game.

    NOTE: In conversation, you may hear the following short forms. You should never write these forms, but you will hear native speakers use them in conversation.

    could have   You will hear *coulda.*
    must have   You will hear *musta.*

    In addition, do not write *could of, may of, might of,* or *must of* for these forms.

3. **Negative sentences**

    RULE: Add the word *not* after the first auxiliary.

    She *may not have been* in an accident. She *might not have hurt* herself while playing sports.

    He *must not have broken* his ankle during the game. They *could not (couldn't*) have had* an accident with the car.

Follow this pattern for negative sentences using *could, may, might,* and *must* for past possibility or probability:

subject	auxiliary	not	auxiliary (have)	verb (past participle)	
She	may	not	have	been	in an accident.
She	might	not	have	hurt	herself.
He	must	not	have	broken	his ankle.
They	could	not	have	had	an accident.

NOTE: We do not use *had to* in the negative for past probability.

---

*Contractions are often used in conversation. They are not usually used in formal writing.

4. *Could not have* means impossible, so it is stronger than *may not have* or *might not have* in the negative.

| might not have | may not have | must not have | could not have |

> She *may not/might not have been* in an accident. (possibility/perhaps)
>
> They *could not have had* an accident with the car. That's impossible. They were not in the car all day.

5. **Questions**

Usually we use only *could* in questions about past possibility.

RULE: Place the first auxiliary to the left of the subject of the sentence.

a. **Yes/no questions**

> *Could* she *have had* an accident? *Could* he *have broken* his ankle?

Follow this pattern for yes/no questions using *could* for past possibility:

auxiliary	subject	auxiliary *(have)*	verb (past participle)	
Could	she	have	had	an accident?
Could	he	have	broken	his ankle?

b. **Question word questions**

Place the question word and the first auxiliary to the left of the subject.

> *How could* she *have had* an accident? *Where could* he *have broken* his ankle?

Follow this pattern for question word questions using *could* for past possibility:

question word	auxiliary	subject	auxiliary *(have)*	verb (past participle)	
How	could	she	have	had	an accident?
Where	could	he	have	broken	his ankle?

Practice

Activity 1

Match each statement in the column on the left with the possibility or probability from the column on the right.

A.

_____ 1. Jane has been sneezing all day.

_____ 2. John's instructor excused his absence.

_____ 3. When I woke up this morning, the cut on my finger was red and sore.

_____ 4. The ambulance took away the driver of the car after the accident.

_____ 5. I accidentally slammed the car door on my hand.

a. It may have become infected.

b. She must have needed medical attention.

c. He might have shown her a note from his doctor.

d. That had to have hurt quite a bit.

e. Her allergies could have started up again.

B.

_____ 1. Betty said she was sick, but she came to class today.

_____ 2. Greg twisted his ankle yesterday, but last night he ran five miles.

_____ 3. Peter was supposed to get my medicine, but I don't see it anywhere.

_____ 4. Why didn't Sue see the dentist for her toothache today?

_____ 5. My husband said he was calling this pharmacy to refill my prescription.

a. He could not have been in much pain.

b. He might not have had time to go to the pharmacy.

c. There may not have been any open appointments today.

d. He must not have called because we don't have any order for you.

e. She must not have felt too sick to take the test.

Activity 2 *(Review coordinating and subordinating conjunctions: Unit One, pages 42–49 and Unit Two, pages 77–87.)*

Jeremy is studying to be a paramedic, and last night he traveled with an ambulance bringing people to the emergency room of a hospital. He wrote some observations about what he saw in the emergency room in a journal. Find seven mistakes in his journal entry and show how to fix them.

Last night was very interesting for me because I had a chance to work hands-on in an ambulance, and I observed many different people with different problems whenever we went to the emergency room. It could been an unusual night there, but I don't think so.

- I saw a young man about 20 years old with a large cut on his leg. He was carrying his skateboard, so he must had had an accident with it.

- A young woman brought in a small baby. The baby could have not been more than a few weeks old and was crying very loudly. It had to has been very frightening for the woman. She certainly looked very worried.

- I watched a boy about ten years old as he came out of the examination area. He was walking slowly and limping. He may has hurt his foot.

- One woman came in with her husband, but she did not look very sick. I was wondering why she was there. She might not have really need the emergency room.

- I also saw an older man as he entered the room and went quickly to the check-in area. He was holding his chest, and they took him immediately for an examination. He must of had a serious problem because they took him ahead of several other people.

Information for Activities 3 and 4

Alternative Medicine/Therapies

Read the following short descriptions of some alternative kinds of medicine or therapy. This information will help you in the next two activities.

reflexology	applies pressure to the feet to help heal the whole body
	good for stress and relaxing the mind
biofeedback	says our mind can influence the functions of our body
	using a machine with sensors we can learn to control usually involuntary processes such as heart rate, blood pressure, and hand temperature
	also uses relaxation techniques
aromatherapy	treatment using scents from plants/trees such as rose, lavender, and eucalyptus
	takes away tension and fatigue, reduces anxiety, and promotes relaxation
chiropractic	a drugless healing profession based on helping control the nervous system
	a chiropractor manipulates joints of the body, especially the spine
acupuncture	needles are put into certain locations of the body in order to keep the energy flow of the body in balance
	used for many purposes, including preventing disease, relieving pain, and as anesthesia for surgery

Activity 3

Complete each sentence in the following conversations to show past possibility or probability. Use the modal or expression given in parentheses and one of the verbs listed below. Use each verb only once. The first one has been done as an example.

try	agree	go	help	use	see

1. Burt: Did you see Amanda today? She seemed so relaxed all morning.

   Lois: She (might) <u>might have used</u> some aromatherapy. She said
             she was interested in trying it.

2. Lisa: I learned how to control my heart rate and breathing to help me relax.

   Steven: You (must) _____ biofeedback. We read about that in my psychology class last week.

3. Phillip: I saw Barb last week and she said she had an amazing experience with her surgery. She didn't tell me any details, though.

   Pam: She (may) _____ to use acupuncture instead of the usual kind of anesthesia. Her new doctor recommended it, but she was nervous about trying it.

4. Jason: I'm sorry I didn't invite you to come with me for the reflexology session. It was great.

   Max: That's okay. I (could—negative) _____ with you anyway. I was busy preparing a big report. Of course, it probably (could) _____ me relax. I was really stressed out.

5. Jill: Did you see Bob? He was in a lot of pain.

   Ivy: I know. He (must—negative) _____ his chiropractor when you saw him. He said he was trying to make an appointment for today.

Activity 4

Read the short descriptions of some people who tried to use some of the alternative methods and therapies above. Write one or two sentences about possibilities or probabilities to guess which kind(s) of therapy each person tried last week. Include some negative guesses about the therapies you think a person did not try as well.

1. Angela is very sensitive to smell and does not like strong odors. She wanted to find new ways to relax and take away her stress.

    _____

    _____

    _____

    _____

    _____

2. Jack has had problems with a painful shoulder, but he did not want to take any painkillers.

   _____

   _____

   _____

   _____

   _____

3. Cynthia wanted to relax and try to get more energy, but she did not have time to make appointments and visit any practitioners. She wanted to do something at home by herself.

   _____

   _____

   _____

   _____

   _____

4. Randi has always been afraid of needles. She wanted to relax and have more positive energy.

   _____

   _____

   _____

   _____

   _____

Sentence Patterns

Transitive/Intransitive Verbs

[1]**We extract crude oil** from under the Earth's surface. [2]However, **this oil supply will not be available** forever. [3]In fact, **this supply is dwindling.** [4]At our current rate of use, **we may exhaust our supply** of this oil in another 50 to 100 years.

Presentation

Questions

1. Underline the subject and the verb in each of the sentences in the presentation. Circle any objects in these sentences.

2. What is the minimum necessary to make a good sentence in English? Does every sentence in English require a subject, verb, and object?

3. Look at the verbs in sentences 2 and 3. Why is there a form of *be* in each of these sentences? Do these forms (*be* and *is*) act in the same way in both these sentences?

Explanation—Sentence Patterns: Transitive/Intransitive Verbs

subject—verb—object OR subject—verb—no object

1. A common word-order pattern in English is subject—verb—object (SVO). Some verbs require an object. In these cases the subject is making the action and the object is receiving the action. The verb in this kind of sentence is called *transitive*.

We extract crude oil from under the Earth's surface.
S V O

We may exhaust our supply of oil in another 50 to 100 years.
S V O

2. Not every verb will have an object following it. A verb that does not require an object is called *intransitive*.

In fact, *this supply is dwindling*.
S V

Our *oil supplies* may *last* only another 50 to 100 years.
S V

3. Some verbs are always either transitive or intransitive. Other verbs can be used both ways, depending on the meaning and use.

If you are not sure about whether a verb is transitive or intransitive, a dictionary usually indicates this with the letters *t* or *vt* (transitive) and *i* or *vi* (intransitive).

We are depleting our resources.
S V (vt) O

Sometimes soil erodes from overgrazing or overplanting.
S V (vi)

Deforestation can erode soil to make it unusable for farming.
S V(vt) O

Commercial oil drilling began in 1859 in Pennsylvania.
S V (vi)

In 1859 Edwin Drake began oil drilling in Pennsylvania.
S V(vt) O

4. You will not find a subject or object after a preposition. (See Lessons 29 to 31, pages 213–231, for more information about prepositions.)

If you are not sure about the subject or object of a sentence, cross out the prepositions and the nouns/pronouns that follow them.

Many countries ~~in the world~~ face problems ~~with dwindling resources~~.
One ~~of the biggest problems~~ concerns depletion ~~of many natural resources~~.

5. There are three common sentence patterns that do not have an object and have *linking verbs*. (For more information about adjectives see Lesson 32 page 233.) Some common linking verbs are:

be seem appear become feel taste smell look sound

a. Pattern 1: subject—linking verb—adjective

This oil supply will not *be available* forever.
S V ADJ

Some people feel anxious about the limited oil supply, and
S V ADJ

the situation seems difficult to fix.
S V ADJ

b. Pattern 2:   subject—linking verb—noun (of identification)

(For more information about nouns see Lesson 27 page 195.) NOTE: Notice that this one has no commas.

> *Some people have become experts* on the availability of oil supplies.
> S   V   NOUN

> *My friend is an engineer* at an oil company.
> S   V   NOUN

c. Pattern 3:   subject—linking verb—location (with a preposition)

(For more information about prepositions of location see Lesson 29 page 213.)

> *Some people are in various locations* around the world to look for
> S   V   LOCATION (preposition)
> more oil supplies.

> *Oil wells are at many locations* around the world.
> S   V   LOCATION (preposition)

6. Be careful with the word *be*, including all of its parts *(is/am/are/was/were/been)*

Sometimes *be* is the main verb of the sentence when it is a linking verb.

> This oil supply will not *be* available forever. My friend *is* an engineer at an oil company. He has *been* an engineer for many years there.

It can also be an auxiliary when it works with a main verb in the progressive. (See Units 1 and 2 for a review of different progressive tenses.)

> Our oil supply *is dwindling*. We *have been depleting* our supplies of many resources.

Practice

Activity 1

1. *Underline the subject and circle the object (if any) in each of the following sentences.*
2. *Label the verbs as transitive with a* vt *or intransitive with a* vi. *If a sentence has two clauses, label these words in each clause.*

EXAMPLE:
We are extracting (many natural resources) and some of them are
        vt

dwindling to dangerous levels.
    vi

1. The Earth has several resources for energy, such as oil and coal.

2. Renewable resources will replenish themselves over short periods

    of time.

3. Nonrenewable resources form very slowly.

4. We exploit reserves such as crude oil, and many people profit from this.

5. We cannot use the untapped resources immediately, but we know the location of many of them.

6. Some resources exist in large quantities, but we have not used them yet for many reasons.

7. Scientists and engineers go to many areas around the world to look for more exploitable resources.

Activity 2   *(Review coordinating conjunctions: Unit One, pages 8–13.)*

Underline all of the linking verbs in the following sentences. State whether each linking verb is followed by an adjective, a noun, or a preposition. Be sure to check all the clauses in each sentence.

> **EXAMPLE:**   The economic value of reserves <u>is</u> important to us.
> adjective

1. Resources are deposits of natural materials.

2. We can estimate the amount of resources on Earth, but we cannot be sure about these amounts.

3. Some natural resources, such as trees and sunlight, are renewable.

4. Problems with nonrenewable resources seem serious, so we should be careful about using them too much.

5. Some problems are in areas of deforestation or desertification.

6. Many people feel nervous about environmental problems.

7. Some people have become environmentalists, and many people have become active in trying to solve some of our problems.

8. Many people appear upset about our environmental problems, but not all of them take action to help the situation.

9. Some environmentalists are at sites of problems, and they want to help improve the situation.

Activity 3

Underline all the verbs in the following paragraph that include be *or one of its parts* (am/is/are/was/were/been). *Then label each of these as* mv *(main verb or linking verb) or* aux *(auxiliary* be *working with a main verb). The first sentence has been done as an example.*

My best friend's name <u>is</u> Frank, and he <u>is studying</u> at a university near
          mv   aux

my house. He has been a student at this school for several years now, and

he will graduate at the end of this school year. Right now he is also a

research assistant. He is working on plant identification in rain forests in

South America. Some plants are disappearing from those areas, and he

wants to help identify them. Last year he was in Hawaii because he was

conducting similar research on the plants there. He was sorry to see that

many plants there are in danger. This loss of plant life is also affecting the

habitats of some animals. Maybe in the future he will use this research to

help solve the problems before it is too late to help.

Activity 4

A. *Complete the following sentences with any information that makes sense. Label the verbs in your sentences as transitive or intransitive.*

1. World population has become _____ .

2. We have almost exhausted _____ .

3. In some places animals overgraze _____ .

4. Alternative energy, such as hydroelectric power, is _____ .

5. We should not waste _____ .

6. In thinking about today's environmental problems, many people feel

   _____ .

7. Some nonrenewable resources are _____ .

B. *Choose four transitive verbs and four intransitive verbs from the lists below and write a sentence with each one. Each of your sentences should say something about any topic related to the environment.*

Transitive		Intransitive	
replenish	extract	live	happen
exhaust	exploit	stay	exist
deplete	implement	occur	go

_____

_____

_____

_____

_____

_____

_____

_____

_____

_____

_____

_____

_____

_____

_____

_____

_____

_____

_____

_____

_____

_____

_____

_____

Passive Sentences

Introduction with Simple Present/ Simple Past Verbs

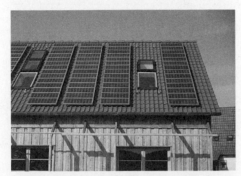

[1]**Renewable alternative energy resources are found** all over the world. [2]**We create energy** from these resources without depleting them. [3]**Such energy is produced** in various countries. [4]**Some of these resources were used by only a few people** in the past, and too many people used nonrenewable resources.

Presentation

Questions

1. Underline the subject in each of the sentences in the presentation.

2. Is the subject doing the action in all of these sentences? If not, in which sentence(s) is the subject doing the action?

3. Circle the verbs in each sentence in the presentation. What is unusual about some of these verbs? Can you explain why they don't all follow the usual pattern of *be* + verb + *-ing*?

4. What is the time in sentence 2 and sentence 4? How do you know this?

Explanation—Passive Sentences—Simple Present/ Simple Past

1. As discussed in Lesson 21, many sentences in English follow the subject— verb—object pattern. The doer of the action, or the *agent,* comes before the verb, and the object follows the verb. These sentences are *active* sentences.

    Few people used these resources in the past.
    S/agent   V   O

2. Sometimes we don't want to focus on the agent. Instead, we want to focus on the object—what the agent does something to or the result of the action. In these situations, the word order follows a different pattern in a sentence. These sentences use the passive voice. We make a *passive* sentence as follows.

Active: Few people used these resources in the past.
            S/agent   V   O

Passive: These resources were used by few people in the past.
            S   V   agent

Notice that the object of the active sentence becomes the subject of the passive sentence.

3. A passive sentence is different from an active sentence in several ways:

a. The subject of a passive sentence is not making the action of the verb. It is not the agent.

   These resources were used by few people in the past.

   Resources cannot use anything. This subject is not making any action in this sentence.

b. The verb of a passive sentence changes to include a form of *be* and the past participle of the main verb.

   These resources *were used* by few people in the past.

   In addition, the verb in the passive sentence will agree with the new subject (the object from the active sentence).

active	passive
Few people *used* these resources in the past.	These resources *were used* by few people in the past.
Few people *used* that resource in the past.	That resource *was used* by few people in the past.

c. If the agent or doer of the action is mentioned, it follows the word *by* and goes after the verb.

   These resources were used *by few people* in the past.

4. In some ways a passive sentence is not different from an active sentence.

a. Both sentences follow the same time/verb tense. Therefore, it is important to pay attention to the verb form and the time of the sentence.

   ACTIVE   Many people *use* such energy in various countries.
                  simple present verb (general time)

   PASSIVE   Such energy *is used* by many people in various countries.
          simple present of *be* + past participle (general time in passive)

   ACTIVE   Few people *used* some of these resources in the past.
                  simple past (past time)

   PASSIVE   Some of these resources *were used* by few people in the past.
         simple past of *be* + past participle (past time in passive)

b. Both sentences have basically the same meaning. The difference between the two sentences may be in emphasis or *focus*. In passive sentences, the object may move to subject position to show more importance than the subject (agent). (See number 5 for more information.)

5. Sometimes we use a passive sentence because we do not know the agent.

Such energy is produced all over the world.

Who produces the energy? We cannot be sure, but it is important to know that it is produced in many places.

It also may not be important or necessary to know or talk about the doer of the action.

Active: People find renewable resources all over the world.

Passive: Renewable resources are found ~~by people~~ all over the world. (no agent necessary)

Active: We create energy from these resources without depleting them.

Passive: Energy is created ~~(by us)~~ from these resources without depleting them.

6. To make passive sentences negative or into questions, follow the same rules discussed previously. (See Unit One and Unit Two in this text.)

a. **RULE:** For negative sentences place *not* after the auxiliary.

subject	auxiliary	not	past participle	
Such energy	*is*	*not*	*used*	by many people in various countries.
Some of these resources	*were*	*not*	*used*	by people in the past.

b. **RULE:** For yes/no questions, place the auxiliary to the left of the subject.

auxiliary	subject	past participle	
Is	such energy	*used*	by many people in various countries?
Were	some of these resources	*used*	by people in the past?

c. **RULE:** For question word questions add a question word and place the auxiliary to the left of the subject.

question word	auxiliary	subject	past participle	
How	*were*	some of these resources	*used*	by people in the past?
Why	*are*	so many nonrenewable resources	*used*	so much today?

7. Only sentences with transitive verbs can become passive. If there is no object in a sentence, it cannot be made passive. Look at the following examples. No passive sentence can be made from either of these examples.

Many of our natural resources are dwindling.

vi

Different kinds of renewable resources exist in various places around the world.

vi

8. Be careful about how much you use the passive in your writing. Many people feel writers should use active sentences more often than passive ones in academic writing. You will often see passive sentences in writing about the sciences because in those fields we may not know the agent of an action or do not need to explicitly state who or what makes the action.

> A chemical reaction was created during the experiment in the lab.

Sometimes the result of an action is more important than what made it occur.

> The water is heated underground, and then it is used to help supply energy in the town.

Practice

Activity 1

Label the following sentences active (A) or passive (P). Then do two things:

A. *State who or what is making the action (the agent). If this information is not in the sentence, write the word* unknown.

B. *State whether the time of the sentence is general time (simple present verb) or past time (simple past verb).*

EXAMPLES:

___A___ In the past some people used a few renewable resources.

agent: _people_____   time: _past (simple past verb)_____

___P___ Renewable resources are replenished in a relatively short amount of time.

agent: _unknown_____

time: _general (simple present verb-passive)_____

_____ 1. People in Iceland use clean energy from heat beneath the surface of the land.

agent: _____

time: _____

_____ 2. Steam from heated water is driven by electric generators to provide energy.

agent: _____

time: _____

_____ 3. Geothermal energy is produced easily because of Iceland's location in a "hot spot."

agent: _____

time: _____

_____ 4. People started using geothermal energy in 1904.

   agent: _____

   time: _____

_____ 5. Centuries ago human use of wind power was created in the
          Netherlands.

   agent: _____

   time: _____

_____ 6. Even nowadays power is still made by windmills in that country.

   agent: _____

   time: _____

_____ 7. Windmills pump ground water to provide energy.

   agent: _____

   time: _____

_____ 8. A constant, forceful flow of wind is required for successful wind
          power.

   agent: _____

   time: _____

Activity 2

Complete the following passive sentences using the correct form of the verb for the time of the sentence. The first one in each section has been done as an example. Some are negative.

A. _Past time (Put all verbs in simple past for passive.)_

1. In early civilizations power <u>was developed</u> from available natural resources.
                                  develop

2. For example, animal power _____ for farming and carrying
    heavy loads.   use

3. In addition, energy _____ from wind and falling water.
                         make

4. Boats and large ships _____ by the wind.
                          power

5. These ships _____ by the sun.
                 not / power

6. The power of rivers and falling water _____ by wooden water
    wheels.   utilize

B.   *General time (Put all verbs in simple present for passive.)*

1.   These days energy <u>is produced</u> in many different ways all over the world.
           produce

2.   Nowadays falling water _____ to make electricity in
     hydroelectric facilities.   use

3.   Usually dams _____ in order to create hydroelectric energy.
                      build

4   However, the ecosystem frequently _____ by dams.
                                        damage

5.   Sometimes animal habitats _____ by dams.
                                 destroy

Activity 3

First, indicate on the line next to each number whether the time of the sentence is general/habitual with **gen** *or past with* **past**. *Then, decide whether the sentence is active or passive and fill in the space with the correct form of the verb given.*

EXAMPLE:

<u>past</u> Some people <u>found</u> a few renewable resources many years ago.
                        find

_____   1.   In the past people _____ only some of the world's
                                   use
              hydroelectric potential.

_____   2.   For anyone to use tidal power for energy, a big difference
              between high and low tides _____ .
                                           need

_____   3.   Through tidal power, electric generators _____
              pollution-free energy.   produce

_____   4.   Before a few years ago almost no tidal-power facilities
              _____ by power companies.
                construct

_____   5.   Even these days very few tidal-power facilities _____ .
                                                                exist

Activity 4   *(Review conjunctions and transitions: Unit Four, pages 111–120.)*

Find six mistakes in the following paragraph and show how to fix them. Be sure to remove any agents that may be unnecessary in passive sentences.

Nonrenewable natural resources used today in many places, but they are limited in availability. They are extracted from the Earth by people at an alarming rate; however, they are replenished not. This is because they form slowly over many, many years. Fossil fuels, such as oil and coal, is burned to provide heat and energy. However, pollution is creating from these materials, and someday the supplies of these materials will run out. Therefore, we need to find good alternatives for these particular resources as soon as possible. We should explore the use of renewable resources so that clean, cheap energy is produce without destroying the environment.

Activity 5

A. *Change each of the following sentences from active to passive. You may leave out the agent in the passive sentence if you think it is not necessary. If no passive sentence is possible, write* NO CHANGE.

1. The sun provides renewable energy.

    _____

    _____

2. Solar power creates electricity in some places.

    _____

    _____

3. Last year we installed solar panels on our roof.

    _____

    _____

4. Our roof was strong enough to hold several panels.

    _____

    _____

5. This past winter we did not use our water heater very much because of the solar energy.

_____

_____

6. The water heater is in our basement to use if necessary.

_____

_____

B. *Change each of the following sentences from passive to active. If the passive sentence has no agent, use the word "people" or "we" for your subject.*

1. In the past our energy needs were provided by a few renewable resources.

_____

_____

2. For example, some kinds of transportation were powered by steam.

_____

_____

3. Some homes around the world are heated by wood.

_____

_____

4. Animal dung is not used as much as wood for heating.

_____

_____

5. In sunny climates solar power is used for heating.

_____

_____

Passive Sentences

Progressive and Perfect Verb Tenses

[1]**Has progress been made** in the last 15 to 20 years regarding environmental issues? [2]At the Earth summit in 2002, **some signs** of environmental progress **were found,** and today **more work is being done** to continue that progress.

Presentation

Questions

1. Which of the sentences in the presentation are passive? How do you know this?

2. What is the time in each of these sentences? Be prepared to explain your answers.

Explanation—Passive Voice Sentences—Progressive and Perfect Tenses

1. As discussed in Lesson 22 (page 160), passive sentences are formed by moving the object of an active sentence to subject position and changing the verb to include *be* + past participle. The verb in the passive sentence remains in the same tense as the active sentence.

> At the Earth summit in 2002, representatives *found* some signs of progress.

> At the Earth summit in 2002, some signs of progress *were found*.

2. Lesson 22 addressed passive sentences with simple past and simple present verb forms. Passive sentences can be made with various other verb forms as well.

verb form	active	passive
Present progressive	We *are making* progress with the problems.	Progress *is being made* with the problems.
Past progressive	We *were making* progress before the summits.	*Progress* was being made before the summits.
Present perfect	We *have made* progress since the first summit in 1992.	Progress *has been made* since the first summit in 1992.
Past perfect	We *had made* progress before we held the summits.	Progress *had been made* before we held the summits.

3. To make these passive sentences negative or questions, follow the same rules discussed in previous units. (See Unit One and Unit Two in this text.)

a. **RULE:** For negative sentences place *not* after the first auxiliary.

subject	auxiliary	not	auxiliary + past participle	
Progress	*is*	*not*	*being made*	with the problems.
Progress	*was*	*not*	*being made*	before the summits.
Progress	*has*	*not*	*been made*	since the first summit in 1992.
Progress	*had*	*not*	*been made*	before we held the summits.

b. **RULE:** For yes/no questions, place the first auxiliary to the left of the subject.

auxiliary	subject	auxiliary + past participle	
Is	progress	*being made*	with the problems?
Was	progress	*being made*	before the summits?
Has	progress	*been made*	since the first summit in 1992?
Had	progress	*been made*	before we held the summits?

c. **RULE:** For question word questions add a question word and place the first auxiliary to the left of the subject.

question word	auxiliary	subject	auxiliary + past participle	
How	*is*	progress	*being made*	with the problems?
When w	*as*	progress	*being made*	before the summits?
Where	*has*	progress	*been made*	since the first summit in 1992?
How	*had*	progress	*been made*	before we held the summits?

In *what* questions, *what* is the subject and comes before the auxiliary.

what (as subject)	auxiliary	auxiliary + past participle	
What	is	being done	to make progress?
What	has	been done	to improve the environment?

Practice

Activity 1

Indicate whether the following sentences are active (A) or passive (P). If a sentence has two clauses, indicate this for each clause. Then state on the line that follows the sentence whether the verb of each clause is simple past, present progressive, past progressive, present perfect, or past perfect.

_____ 1. Representatives from many countries were discussing environmental problems at the two summits. _____

_____ 2. Since then some promises have been kept about helping the environment. _____

_____ 3. Some people have also promoted sustainable development to help human welfare. _____

_____ 4. People wanted to do something to help because they had become more aware of the problems at these summits. _____ _____ (two clauses)

_____ 5. At the summit in 2002, they found that some steps had been taken to improve the problems before they met. _____ _____ (two clauses)

_____ 6. Many possible solutions were being discussed during the various meetings at the summits. _____

_____ 7. Now many people are still trying to find new solutions to environmental problems. _____

_____ 8. In fact, new plans of action are being suggested and implemented even today. _____

Activity 2

Fill in the spaces of the passive sentences below with the correct form of the verb from the active sentence. Do not change the tense of the verb.

1. Discussions at summit meetings have educated people about environmental problems.

   People _____ by discussions at summit meetings about environmental problems.

2. After representatives had discussed some ideas at the first summit, they held other conferences.

   After some ideas _____ at the first summit, other

   conferences _____ .

3. In the past some of our industrial practices were polluting the air and water.

   In the past the air and water _____ by some of our industrial practices.

4. Some power plants were emitting large amounts of harmful chemicals in the air.

   Large amounts of harmful chemicals _____ in the air by some power plants.

5. For years before the summits, these power plants had not reduced the emissions of dangerous chemicals.

   For years before the summits, the emissions of dangerous chemicals

   _____ .

6. Since the summits, people have gained a new sensitivity to our impact on the environment.

   A new sensitivity to our impact on the environment _____ since the summits.

7. Many people are now making changes in their lifestyle in order to help the environment.

   Changes in lifestyle _____ by many people in order to help the environment.

8. More and more people are driving hybrid cars, for example.

   Hybrid cars _____ by more and more people, for example.

Activity 3

Find eight mistakes with verb forms in the following paragraph and show how to fix them.

What kinds of emissions has caused problems to the environment, and what being done about these problems now? Chlorinated chemicals were be used freely in many countries for many years. At a United Nations conference in Stockholm in 2001, a treaty was adopted by many countries to control the use of these chemicals. Before that time they had cause much pollution in the air and water. Our air and water have also been harm by emissions from automobiles and other forms of transportation. These vehicles were emitting too much harmful exhaust because they was being powered by gas and oil. Before the second Earth Summit in 2002, an agreement had be made at a conference in Kyoto to reduce those emissions. Many countries support this agreement, but the United States' support has been withdrew.

Activity 4

Change the active sentences below to passive and the passive ones to active. a. When you change from active to passive, include the agent (with by*) only if you think it is necessary. b. If a passive sentence has no agent, use* people *or* we *for the subject of your active sentence. c. If the sentence is active and cannot change to passive, write* NO CHANGE.

1. Corrective actions to "think green" have been taken by many people.

2. Many industrialized nations were discussing environmental problems at the conferences.

3. Before hybrid cars most automobiles had used only gas to run.

4. Today hybrid cars are being made by several car manufacturers.

5. Some companies have designed cars to use hydrogen fuel cells for power.

6. Ecotourism has become more popular in recent years.

7. Before ecotourism many tourists had not preserved the environment on their vacations.

8. Vacations were being taken without regard for the local people and the land.

9. These days travelers are considering the impact of their visit on the local area.

10. Many people travel to distant places to learn about the culture of the area.

Activity 5

Discuss the following with a partner. Share your answers with a group or with your class.

What environmental problems does your local community face? What environmental problems does your country face? What has been done to work on these problems? What is being done to solve these problems?

Passive with Modals

Presentation 1

Questions

1. Circle the modals in all of the sentences in the presentation. Put a line under the verbs and auxiliaries that follow these modals.

2. What is the same for all of the auxiliaries and verbs that follow the modals? What is the pattern for using modals and passive together?

3. How can you make these sentences negative?

[1]What **can be done** by ordinary people to help the environment? [2]Simple steps **should be taken** in our everyday lives to help solve some of the problems. [3]The Earth **must be given** a chance to renew itself and recover from some of its problems. [4]If people start to think green more consistently, perhaps humanity's impact on the environment **will be lessened.**

Explanation—Passive with Modals

1. In Unit One you learned about using the modal *will* and expression *be going to* for the future. In Unit 3 you learned about the meanings of other modals and their equivalent expressions. We can use these words and expressions in passive sentences as well as active ones. Follow this pattern to use modals and equivalent expressions in passive sentences: subject (not the agent) + modal (equivalent expression) + *be* + verb (past participle)

Choose the modal or equivalent expression according to the meaning you want for your sentence.

future (prediction or certainty)	Humanity's impact on the environment *will be lessened.* Humanity's impact on the environment *is going to be lessened.*
necessity	The Earth *must be given* a chance to renew itself. The Earth *has got to be given* a chance to renew itself.
advice	Simple steps *should be taken* to help solve the problems. Simple steps *ought to be taken* to help solve the problems.
stronger advice	Simple steps *had better be taken* to help solve the problems.
possibility	Humanity's impact on the environment *might be lessened.* Humanity's impact on the environment *may be lessened.* Humanity's impact on the environment *could be lessened.*
ability	Several steps *can be taken* by each person.

2. To make these passive sentences negative or questions, follow the same rules discussed in previous units.

   a. **RULE:** For negative sentences place *not* after the first auxiliary.

subject	auxiliary + not	auxiliary + past participle
Humanity's impact on the environment	*will not*	*be lessened.*
Humanity's impact on the environment	*is not*	*going to be lessened.*
Negative actions	*must not*	*be increased* in order to help solve the problems.
Humanity's impact on the environment	*might not*	*be lessened.*

   b. **RULE:** For yes/no questions, place the first auxiliary to the left of the subject.

auxiliary	subject	auxiliary + past participle
Will	humanity's impact on the environment	*be lessened?*
Is	humanity's impact on the environment	*going to be lessened?*
Should	negative actions	*be decreased* in order to help solve the problems?
Could	humanity's impact on the environment	*be decreased?*

   c. **RULE:** For question word questions add a question word and place the first auxiliary to the left of the subject.

question word	auxiliary	subject	auxiliary + past participle
How	*will*	humanity's impact on the environment	*be lessened?*
When	*is*	humanity's impact on the environment	*going to be lessened?*
Where	*could*	humanity's impact on the environment	*be decreased?*
Why	*should*	negative actions	*be decreased?*

Practice

Activity 1   (*Review conjunctions and transitions: Unit Four, pages 111–120.*)

Match each clause in the column on the left with the clause that best completes it from the column on the right. Use each answer only one time.

_____ 1. If everyone recycles paper, glass, and plastic goods,

a. they had better not be wasted.

_____ 2. We continue to use more and more oil; as a result,

b. bad emissions from vehicles can be lessened.

_____ 3. Since nonrenewable resources are not unlimited,

c. damage to the ozone could be increased with their use.

_____ 4. More people are learning about ecotourism; therefore,

d. the amount of garbage will be reduced.

_____ 5. Solar power should be used in more ways because

e. our supplies of it are going to be more depleted.

_____ 6. If people use more public transportation or car pools,

f. supplies of fossil fuels might not be exhausted so quickly.

_____ 7. We need to be careful about our use of certain chemicals, for

g. that source of energy is renewable.

_____ 8. Alternative forms of transportation and heating should be used, so

h. some native cultures and natural areas could be protected.

Activity 2

Fill in each blank space with the modal given and one of the verbs listed below in the passive. Use each verb only one time. Be sure to make your answer negative if indicated.

adopt	reduce	exploit	manufacture	hold

1. Alternative types of cars (can) _____ ; therefore, we could use less gas.

2. More conferences among many nations for global cooperation (could) _____ .

3. More treaties to control the use of damaging chemicals (ought to) _____ .

4. The amount of damaging emissions (must) _____ as soon as possible.

5. Furthermore, our nonrenewable resources (should—negative) _____ at such a high rate.

 Activity 3

Find nine mistakes in the following conversation and show how to correct them.

Marilyn: I've been doing some research about our use of oil and how our economy can be affect by this. Can you guess how many millions of barrels of oil is consumed each day?

Bruce: I don't know much about that. Could be more than 5 million barrels a day used?

Marilyn: Actually it's already more than 80 million barrels a day. That much is need because we use it for energy in so many areas of our daily lives. For example, energy must is used by agriculture to produce food.

Bruce: Also, I guess the food has to shipped by various forms of transportation, and they use energy too.

Marilyn: That's right. You might be surprise by how many goods are shipped to stores and businesses every day.

Bruce: Don't forget many homes not are heated by wood, and they also depend on oil for heat in winter. I see what you mean about our economy now. If we deplete our oil supplies too much, many areas of our lives is going to be touched by shortages.

Presentation 2

Modals in the Past with Passive

[1]Today we are experiencing many problems with our environment. [2]Perhaps in the past more conferences and summits **should have been held** by as many nations as possible. [3]Thus, stricter laws and regulations **could have been enacted** by many countries. [4]The seriousness of the situation **must not have been understood** until more recently.

Questions

1. Which of these sentences are active and which are passive? How do you know?

2. What is the time in sentences 2, 3, and 4? How many auxiliaries do you see with the verbs in each of those sentences?

3. Look at sentence 4 and state the rule for making a sentence with more than one auxiliary negative.

Explanation—Modals in the Past with Passive

1. As you learned in Lessons 19 and 20 in Unit Three in this text, some modals can be used in the past as follows:

    should/ought to/could/might + *have* + verb = past regret

    Something was a good idea in the past but it was not done.

    > Governments *should have held* more conferences about environmental problems.

    might/may/could/must + *have* + verb = past possibility or probability

    These words show different degrees of certainty with *must* the strongest and most probable.

    > We *might have seen* the start of these problems many years ago. Some people *must have understood* the seriousness of these problems.

2. We also sometimes use these modals in the past with passive.

    > Perhaps in the past more conferences and summits *should have been held* by as many nations as possible.

    > Thus, stricter laws and regulations *could have been enacted* by many countries.

    > At first the problems *must have been considered* less serious.

3. Be sure to include all of the necessary auxiliaries and to use their correct forms.

    modal + *have* (simple form) + *been* (past participle after *have*) + verb (past participle in passive)

4. To make these passive sentences negative or questions, follow the same rules discussed in previous units.

a. **RULE:** For negative sentences place *not* after the first auxiliary.

subject	auxiliary	not	passive auxiliary (have been)	past participle	
The seriousness of the situation	*must*	*not*	*have been*	*understood*	until more recently.
More conferences and summits	*should*	*not*	*have been*	*held*	by as many nations as possible.
Stricter laws	*could*	*not*	*have been*	*enacted*	by many countries. and regulations

b. **RULE:** For yes/no questions, place the first auxiliary to the left of the subject.

auxiliary	subject	passive auxiliary (have been)	past participle	
Should	more conferences and summits	*have been*	*held*	by as many nations as possible?
Could	stricter laws and regulations	*have been*	*enacted*	by many countries?

c. **RULE:** For question word questions add a question word and place the first auxiliary to the left of the subject.

question word	auxiliary	subject	passive auxiliary (have been)	past participle	
When	*should*	more conferences and summits	*have been*	*held?*	
How	*could*	stricter laws and regulations	*have been*	*enacted*	by many countries?

Activity 4

Read each statement and then write True (T) or False (F) for each sentence that follows. The first one has been done as an example.

1. Stricter laws about overfishing should have been required in the past.
    __F__ Laws in the past were quite strict.

2. Alternative forms of transportation could have been considered before the oil crisis began.
    _____ We did a good job of considering alternative forms of transportation before the oil crisis.

3. Harmful emissions must have been allowed to pollute our air.
    _____ There were probably few or no laws about harmful emissions going into the air.

4. Certain areas of the ocean ought to have been closed to fishing years ago.
    _____ Areas of the ocean have been closed to fishing for many years.

5. Years ago ecotourism must not have been considered by travelers.
    _____ The idea of ecotourism is probably a fairly new one.

Activity 5

John made some changes to his house in order to conserve energy. Below is a list of things that he possibly or probably did to his house. Fill in each space with the modal and verb given. Use the past passive form in each case and use negative if indicated.

EXAMPLE:

The house (should make) <u>should have been made</u> more energy efficient years ago.

1. Many different places in his house (must check) _____ before any changes were made.

2. The heating system (could inspect) _____ to make sure it was running as cleanly and efficiently as possible.

3. A new thermostat (may install) _____ so he could be sure his house is kept at an energy-efficient temperature.

4. Drafts on windows and doors (may eliminate) _____ so that cold air outside cannot enter the house.

5. Weather-stripping (might use) _____ on his windows to make them airtight.

6. However, the insulation in his attic (should replace—negative) _____ because it was brand new.

Activity 6

Read the following regrets about what was not done about the traffic and parking problems in one city. Find six mistakes in the grammar and fix them.

1. Public transportation should has been improved in the downtown area.

2. Ride sharing and car pooling to that area could have be encouraged.

3. More parking structures ought have been built to accommodate more cars.

4. Cars might have banned from the most congested areas. Then those streets could have been reserve for pedestrians only.

5. The rising population and increase in the use of cars must have not been considered by the city planners.

Activity 7

A. *Change the following sentences from active to passive if possible. If this is not possible, write* NO CHANGE.

1. Sometimes waste products from factories could create pollution in rivers and streams.

   _____

2. Overpopulation might affect people's health and food supply in some places.

   _____

3. We have to slow down our loss of wetlands.

   _____

4. We ought to feel responsible for taking care of our environment.

   _____

5. More careful fishing can decrease the loss of coral in our seas.

   _____

6. Use of nuclear reactors is going to make more radioactive waste.

   _____

7. Cities could have implemented strategies for controlling traffic in downtown areas.

   _____

8. Power companies might have utilized more renewable resources for energy supplies.

   _____

9. City governments should not have accepted new building plans without environmental impact reports.

   _____

B. *Change the following sentences from passive to active. If there is no agent in the passive sentence, use* we *for the subject of the active sentence.*

1. Air pollution can be caused by too many vehicles in large cities.

   _____

2. The greenhouse effect will be increased by the continued burning of fossil fuels.

   _____

3. Our wetlands had better not be destroyed at such an alarming rate.

_____

4. The flow of rivers should not be changed by new large dams.

_____

5. Some marine areas must be closed in order to protect them from overfishing.

_____

6. Global warming could have been slowed down by banning the use of certain chemicals.

_____

7. Fewer fossil fuels might have been used with more alternative types of transportation.

_____

8. Our nonrenewable resources should not have been exploited so much.

_____

Activity 8

A. Look at the following list of environmental problems:

> • air and water pollution   • use of nonrenewable resources
> • deforestation   • overfishing/loss of coral reefs
> • damage to the ozone   • global warming/greenhouse effect

1. Work with a partner or in small groups and discuss the causes and effects of one or two of these problems. Also discuss any possible solutions to them.

2. Write one or two passive sentences about the problems you discussed as follows:

    a. Make some predictions about the future effects of these problems. Use will and/or be going to in your sentences.

    b. State some actions you think are necessary to take in order to help solve these problems. Use must/have to in your sentences.

    c. Give some advice about how to solve these problems. Use should/ought to/had better in your sentences.

    d. Write some sentences about possible results of actions we take to solve these problems. Use can/could/might in these sentences.

B. Look back at the list of problems in part A and answer the following questions in complete sentences. Your answers will be guesses and opinions, so no one particular answer is going to be correct for each one.

1. Which problem should have been examined or discussed first? Why?

    _____

    _____

2. Which problem must have been discovered before the others?

    _____

    _____

3. Which problem(s) might have been avoided by the use of alternative transportation?

    _____

    _____

4. Which problem(s) may have been discussed as very serious for the rain forests? Why?

    _____

    _____

5. Which problems could have been decreased or slowed down in the last 20 to 30 years? Explain how this could have been accomplished.

    _____

    _____

Conditional Sentences: Unreal If

Present and General Time

[1]How **would individuals help** the environment **if they changed** their everyday habits? [2]**If each person were** more aware of his/her impact on the environment, **we could minimize** our negative effects. [3]**If we all tried** to be "green thinking," **we would live** in a more environmentally friendly way. [4]For example, **we might lower** the bad emissions in the air **if we used** fewer fossil fuels in our everyday transportation.

Presentation

Questions

1. How many clauses do you see in each of the sentences to the left? In sentences 1 and 4, what word is putting those clauses together? What is the meaning of this word in these sentences?

2. What form of the verbs do you see in the dependent clauses (the *if* clause) of sentences 3 and 4? What auxiliaries do you see with the verbs in the independent clauses of these two sentences? What do you think is the time of these sentences? How can you tell?

3. What form of the verb do you see in the *if* clause of sentence 2? Why is this unusual? What do you think is the time of this sentence?

Explanation—Unreal Conditions with *if*—Present/General Time

1. In *Destinations 2: Writing for Academic Success* you learned about using the subordinating conjunction *if* for sentences with a condition and result. (See Unit Four, Part Three.)

   If *we continue* to use so much oil, we *will (might)* completely *deplete* our reserves of it.

This sentence expresses something that is a real possibility. It is a result that will or might happen in the future if a certain condition is met.

2. Sometimes we use the subordinating conjunction if to talk about something that is not a true situation or a real possibility but is just our imagination. We call these *unreal if* sentences or sometimes *contrary-to-fact* sentences because they are not true or they are impossible.

> *If we all tried* to be more "green thinking," *we would live* in a more environmentally friendly way.
>
> *We might lower* the bad emissions in the air *if we used* fewer fossil fuels in our everyday transportation.

These sentences are unreal because not all people try to be "green thinking," and in general, we don't use fewer fossil fuels in our everyday transportation. Therefore, we can only imagine about these situations.

Sometimes an *unreal if* sentence expresses something impossible.

> *If everyone stopped* using cars immediately, *we would lower* the bad emissions in our air.

It is impossible to get everyone to stop using cars immediately, so we can only imagine about this situation and its results.

3. In these sentences we must make some unusual changes with the verbs as follows:

> *If we all tried* to be more "green thinking," *we would live* in a more environmentally friendly way.

a. The verb in the *if* clause takes the past tense form. However, the time is not the past. In this case the time is present or general/habitual time.
b. We use the modal *would, could,* or *might* with the verb in the independent clause. Choose the modal that fits best for the meaning you want:

> would = probably   could = possibly   might = possibly/small chance

Follow the grammar rules you learned for modals and the verbs that follow them in Unit Three (see page 91).

4. When *be* is used as the main verb of an *unreal if* clause, always use the form *were* and do not change it for the subject.*

> *If each person were/If more people were* more aware of his/her/their impact on the environment, we could minimize our negative effects.

---

*People often use *was* in informal spoken English after *if*.

Practice

Activity 1

Read each statement and then write True (T) or False (F) for each sentence that follows. The first one has been done as an example.

1. If people were more "green thinking," we could see the effects of their efforts.

   __T__ People are not "green thinking" enough now.

2. If we found good substitutes for all our depleted resources, we would not worry about shortages.

   _____ We have already found good substitutes for all our depleted resources.

3. Gas wouldn't be so expensive if fossil fuels were renewable.

   _____ Fossil fuels are renewable.

4. If we developed more ways to use renewable resources for power, we might have lower energy costs.

   _____ We don't have many ways to use renewable resources right now.

5. If we used only renewable resources for energy, we would not have to think about running out of these resources.

   _____ We use only renewable resources for our energy.

6. If cars didn't run on gas, we wouldn't have to worry about the availability of oil reserves.

   _____ We don't have to worry about oil reserves for fuel for our cars.

Activity 2

Complete the following ideas about how people could keep water clean by making each sentence unreal if. *Use the verb given to fill in each space. Use the negative where indicated.*

1. We would keep our water clean or less polluted if we (take)

   _____ shorter showers.

2. If people (take—negative) _____ too many baths or (limit)

   _____ the amount of water in their baths, they could help keep

   water clean.

3. If each person (fix) _____ any leaky faucets in the house, this

   would preserve more clean water.

4. We could help keep the water supply clean if we (join) _____
   clean-up groups at beaches or rivers and streams.

5. Our water supply would stay cleaner if people (throw—negative)
   _____ pollutants such as household cleaners or paint down the
   drain.

6. If each person (be) _____ more willing to do his/her share, the
   water supply might be cleaner in some places.

Activity 3   *(Review coordinating and subordinating conjunctions: Unit One, pages 8–13
and Unit Two, pages 42–49.)*

*Next to each number below you will find problems about people's use of water
and solutions in the form of* unreal if *sentences. Find one mistake in grammar in
each* unreal if *sentence and fix it. Be sure each sentence remains in the* unreal if.

1. People waste water when they brush their teeth. If they didn't let the
   water run so much, they will save a lot of water.

   _____

   _____

2. People often take long, hot showers. We would save water and use less
   heating if each person was more concerned with the amount of hot
   water in the shower.

   _____

   _____

3. Many people take a bath every day, and they often overfill the tub with
   water. If everyone took a shower instead of a bath, she/he would
   protects our water supply and lower our water bills.

   _____

   _____

4. Many people waste water by watering their lawns too much. They could
   save water if they don't overwater their lawns.

   _____

   _____

5. Pollutants and toxic materials in the trash go into landfills, and then they
   can reach the water supply underground. If we didn't put these
   materials in the trash, they don't go into landfills.

   _____

   _____

Activity 4   *(Review dependent/independent clauses: Unit Two, pages 43–44.)*

Complete the following sentences with the form of the verb in parentheses in the
if clause and could, would, *or* might *with the verb given in the independent*
clause. Make the sentence negative where indicated.

1. If all natural resources (be) _____ renewable, they (replenish)

   _____ themselves naturally.

2. If people (use) _____ less oil, our present supply (last)

   _____ longer.

3. If the Earth's resources (be) _____ unlimited, we

   (face—negative) _____ future shortages.

4. Some areas of land (be) _____ more renewable if people

   (deplete—negative) _____ nutrients from the soil (such as

   through overplanting).

5. Some metals (be) _____ renewable if we (recycle)

   _____ them for reuse.

6. If people (become) _____ more knowledgeable about the

   Earth's resources and their availability, we (protect) _____ our

   global environment more.

7. If each country (be) _____ able to manage its industrial

   development more efficiently, we (waste—negative) _____ so

   many natural resources.

Activity 5   *(Review dependent/independent clauses: Unit Two, pages 43–44.)*

The following information is about the reality of geothermal energy and its
use and availability.

> • Only some places on Earth have "hot spots" that are capable of
>   producing geothermal energy.
> • Geothermal energy is relatively nonpolluting and inexpensive.
> • Geothermal energy cannot be transported from one place
>   to another.

Fill in the spaces of the following unreal sentences about geothermal energy with the verb given in the if *clause and your own verb and modal in the independent clause.*

1. If more places on Earth (have) _____ "hot spots," we

    _____ more geothermal energy.

2. If more cities (produce) _____ geothermal energy, they

    _____ relatively pollution free.

3. If more places (use) _____ geothermal energy, those places

    _____ cheaper electricity costs.

4. If geothermal energy (be) _____ easy to transport from one

    place to another, more countries _____ it.

Activity 6

Imagine the opposite situation of what you read in the following pairs of sentences. Then use the information in both sentences given to make one unreal if *sentence. Follow the example.*

1. Factories send smoke into the air. Then they pollute it.

    If factories didn't send smoke into the air, they wouldn't pollute it.

2. People destroy large areas of forest. They cause deforestation problems.

    _____

    _____

3. Some people don't limit their use of carbon-based chemicals. They damage the ozone layer.

    _____

    _____

4. Many natural resources are not renewable. We have problems with energy supplies.

    _____

    _____

5. Building dams disrupts ecosystems. We don't use much hydroelectric power.

    _____

    _____

Conditional Sentences: Unreal If

Past Time

[1]If we **had been** more careful with our environment, we **wouldn't have caused** so many problems. [2]For example, we **could have kept** our waterways cleaner if we **had not allowed** factories to throw waste into them. [3]If we **had made** a bigger effort to keep lakes and rivers clean, we **might not have** so many polluted waterways today.

Presentation

Questions

1. How many clauses do you see in each of the sentences below the photograph on the left? What word connects the clauses? Are these sentences expressing real situations?

2. What form of the verbs do you see in the dependent clauses (the *if* clause) of all three sentences? What auxiliaries do you see with the verbs in the independent clauses of sentences 1 and 2? What is the time in sentences 1 and 2?

Explanation—Unreal Conditionals with *if*—Past Time

1. You learned in Lesson 25 about using the unreal *if* for situations in present or general time. We also use unreal *if* sentences to talk about situations in the past.

    If we *had been* more careful with our environment, we *wouldn't have caused* so many problems.

    (In truth, we were not very careful, so we caused problems.)

We *could have kept* our waterways cleaner if we *had not allowed* factories to throw waste into them.

(In truth, we did not keep our waterways clean because factories did throw waste into them.)

We can use the unreal *if* in the past to express the opposite of the truth and we imagine the opposite results in the past.

2. In these sentences we must make some changes with the verbs as follows:

   If we *had been* more careful with our environment, we *wouldn't have caused* so many problems

   a. The verb in the *if* clause takes the past perfect form.
   b. We add the modal *would, could,* or *might* with the verb in the independent clause followed by *have* and the past participle of the verb.

3. Sometimes we may want to talk about a situation that happened in the past and had an effect on a situation that still exists today. In this case it is possible to use the unreal *if* in the past and to have the unreal result in the present. If we had done something differently in the past, our situation might be different today.

   If we *had made* a bigger effort to keep lakes and rivers clean, we *might not have* so many polluted waterways today.

In this sentence we are imagining the opposite of the truth about the past. (In truth, we did not make a big effort to keep waterways clean.) The imaginary result appears in the independent clause. (In truth, we have many polluted waterways today.)

Practice

Activity 1

Read each statement and then write T for True or F for False for each sentence that follows. The first one has been done as an example.

A. Past Situations

1. If we had used our energy resources more wisely, we could have protected our environment more.

   __F__ In the past we used our energy resources wisely.

2. We might not have used so many of our resources so quickly if we had realized how limited they were.

   _____ We used our limited resources too quickly.

3. We would not have faced fuel shortages if we had been more careful with our use of fossil fuels.

   _____ We've never had any fuel shortages.

4. If we hadn't utilized fossil fuels to provide so much energy, we wouldn't have damaged the environment as much.

   _____ Fossil fuels provided a lot of our energy in the past, and that resulted in environmental damage.

5. If representatives from different countries had held Earth summits many years ago, we could have made more progress solving global environmental problems.

   _____ We made as much progress as possible in solving global environmental problems.

B. Past Situations with Results in the Present

1. If we had identified new supplies of our depleted resources, we could use them for energy.

   _____ We have already identified many new supplies of depleted resources.

2. We might see a smaller hole in the ozone if we hadn't created emissions from the use of fossil fuels.

   _____ The ozone has a very small hole in it now.

3. If we had not depleted so many of our resources, we would not have to face fuel shortages now and in the future.

   _____ We do not have to worry about facing fuel shortages.

4. We would have more forests and natural rain forests today if we had not allowed so much deforestation in the past.

   _____ We did not limit deforestation in the past.

5. If we had limited our use and waste of resources, we might not have to think about changing our lifestyles in the future.

   _____ In the past we limited our use and waste of resources.

Activity 2

Match each clause in the column on the left with the clause that best completes it from the column on the right. Use each answer only one time.

_____ 1. If we had created more hydroelectric power,

_____ 2. If we had found a way to transport geothermal energy,

_____ 3. If tidal power had been possible to create in more places,

_____ 4. If we had closed off fishing to more areas of the ocean,

_____ 5. If more farmers had been careful about their agricultural practices,

_____ 6. If we had developed a cheaper way to produce solar energy,

a. we could use this energy in places far from the Earth's "hot spots."

b. we would not see such a big decrease in the fish population.

c. we would have better soil for agriculture today.

d. many warmer areas of the world could use this kind of power.

e. more electricity could have been produced by rivers.

f. we might have produced more energy from this source.

Activity 3

Find one mistake in each of the following sentences and correct it.

1. We might not have create so many environmental problems if consumers had bought more environmentally friendly products in the past.

2. If consumers had insisted on buying only environmentally friendly products, manufacturers would have not produced so many damaging ones.

3. We might not have our present problem with too much garbage if more people have refused to buy products with unrecyclable packaging in the past.

4. If governments have promoted more recycling programs in the past, more citizens could have participated in them.

5. If more recycling centers had be available in the past, people could have developed a habit of recycling their waste by now.

6. We might not have so many overflowing landfills if each person has recycled garbage, such as glass and aluminum.

Activity 4

A. Complete the following sentences using the verb given in past unreal if. Use the negative where indicated.

1. If we (educate) _____ more people about environmental problems in the past, we could have already fixed some of those problems.

2. If we (allow—negative) _____ so many gases in the air, the sun's heat wouldn't have trapped them to create "greenhouse gases."

3. If the hole in the ozone (get—negative) _____ bigger, our oceans wouldn't have become warmer.

4. If the oceans (become—negative) _____ warmer, we might not have lost so much coral.

5. If we (create) _____ fewer greenhouse gases, the Earth would not have such a big problem with global warming today.

B. Complete the following sentences to make all of them unreal if in the past. Use the verb in parentheses in the if clause and could, would, or might with the verb given in the independent clause. Use negative where indicated. The first one has been done as an example.

(Review dependent and independent clauses: Unit Two, pages 43–44.)

1. London (could have) could have had cleaner air without pollution in the

   1200s if people (burn—negative) had not burned so much coal.

2. If Londoners (use—negative) _____ smoky types of coal,

   the pollution problems (might increase—negative) _____ .

3. Londoners (would avoid) _____ getting another tax on

   the coal if the pollution (decrease) _____ or (remain)

   _____ low.

4. If the pollution problems in London (improve) _____ ,

   there (would be) _____ no need for a study of the

   environment.

5. If the Industrial Revolution (begin—negative) _____ at

   the same time as the study of the environment, more people (might pay

   attention to) _____ the report.

6. Some people in London (could live) _____ longer if the

   air quality of London (get) _____ better.

Activity 5

Complete the following unreal if sentences with a complete clause, using the words given as well as some of your own words in your answers. Your answers should be in the past and negative if indicated.

EXAMPLE:

The tourism industry might have developed ecotourism sooner if _____

_____ .

(effects of tourists on the environment)

The tourism industry might have developed ecotourism sooner if <u>people</u> <u>had thought about the effects of tourists on the environment.</u>

1. We might not have so many traffic jams and pollution from cars today if

   _____ .

   (alternative transportation)

2. Wetland areas could continue to provide a good habitat for wildlife if ___

   _____ .

   (destroy these areas—negative)

3. If world population had increased more slowly, _____

   _____ .

   (deplete natural resources—negative)

4. We could have different kinds of transportation today if _____

   _____ .

   (different energy and fuel sources)

5. If fishermen had been more careful around delicate coral reefs, _____

   _____ .

   (lose them—negative)

Activity 6

Read the following newspaper headlines* about environmental problems and the information that follows about the cause. Imagine the opposite of each situation. Write a sentence using unreal if *in the past about the cause and the opposite effect in the headline. The first one has been done as an example.*

1. Parts of world have food shortages. Populations around world grew too fast.

    If the populations of the world hadn't grown so fast, parts of the world would/might not have food shortages.

2. Hole in ozone bigger than expected. We used too many carbon-based chemicals.

    _____

    _____

3. Large areas of Earth at risk of becoming a desert. They have experienced too much deforestation and agricultural soil depletion.

    _____

    _____

4. Cloud of plastic dust spreads throughout environment. People used and threw away many plastic products.

    _____

    _____

5. More carbon dioxide in the atmosphere today than ever before. People burned so much fuel.

    _____

    _____

6. Many animal habitats need protection. Towns, cities, and farms took over natural areas.

    _____

    _____

---

*Newspaper editors often delete words to make headlines shorter. Do not delete words from your sentences.

Nouns and Quantifiers

Count/Non-Count Nouns

¹Various native **cultures** hold many different **beliefs** about the **world** around them. ²Using their **knowledge** of their **environment, people** seek to explain natural **phenomena.** ³Sometimes these **explanations** help provide **stability** in their **lives.**

Presentation 1

Questions

1. Circle the nouns in sentences 1 and 3.

2. Which ones are singular (one) and which ones are plural (more than one)? How do you know?

Explanation—Count/Non-Count Nouns

1. A noun can be a person, place, thing, or idea/concept.

   Various native *cultures* hold many different *beliefs* about the *world* around them.

2. Some nouns are countable (or count). This means you can think of these as individual separate items and count them.

   Various native *cultures* hold many different *beliefs.* They try to create *explanations* of the *world* around them.

3. When these nouns are singular (one), you can use *a* or *an* with them. (See Lesson 28 in this text for a complete explanation of articles.)

   A certain *belief* can help explain *a situation* related to their environment.

4. When these nouns are plural (more than one), they usually have an -s ending.

> Various native *cultures* hold many different *beliefs*.

Some plural nouns have spelling changes. (See Appendix I, page 268.)

> Some *stories* help provide stability in their *lives*.

Some nouns have irregular plural forms and do not use the -s ending. (See Appendix I, page 268.)

> One *person* may believe a particular story about the world, but other *people* may believe something different.

> People may try to explain an unusual *phenomenon*. However, sometimes these *phenomena* may be too difficult to explain.

5. Some nouns are uncountable (or non-count or mass nouns). This means we do not think of these nouns as individual or separate because they are often too small to count or they are substances, activities, or conditions.

a. These nouns cannot be plural and will not have an -s ending. They also will not have *a* or *an* before them. (See Lesson 28 in this text for a complete explanation of articles.)

> When we study something, we gain some *knowledge* about that subject.

b. The verb in the sentence with non-count nouns will be singular.

> *Stability is* important to them.

> Their *knowledge* of the environment *helps* them explain natural phenomena.

The following list shows some non-count nouns in English in groups.

- liquids: coffee/tea/water/milk/soup/oil/gasoline/paint/perfume
- small, granular things: sugar/sand/dirt/dust/rice/salt/pepper/other spices (such as cinnamon)
- materials: gold/cotton/wood/glass/steel/plastic/rubber/coal/wool/soap
- gases: air/hydrogen/pollution/smog/smoke/steam
- some foods: bread/butter/fish/cheese/meat/chicken/beef/lamb
- abstract nouns: knowledge/intelligence/health/truth/honesty/ courage/wealth/poverty/happiness/trouble/luck/fun/life/beauty/ family/education
- subjects: mathematics/physics/economics/biology/psychology/history/ chemistry/engineering/French/Spanish/English/Chinese
- other: advice/communication/information/news/work/homework/ grammar/vocabulary/traffic/transportation/weather/rain/snow/crime/ agriculture/garbage

6. Some non-count nouns are categories or groups of things. The category or group is uncountable, but the individual parts in the group are countable.

Group	Individual Parts
furniture	chairs/tables/lamps/desks
jewelry	necklaces/rings/bracelets/pins

Some other groups are: equipment/fruit/food/money/clothing/makeup/luggage

Practice

Activity 1

Write the plural form of the noun in parentheses in each space.

There were many Native American (tribe) _____ , and they had

different (community) _____ throughout North America. They
2

shared some of the same (concept) _____ regarding (family)
3

_____ and education, and these (belief) _____ were
4   5

shared by both the (man) _____ and (woman) _____ in
6   7

each tribe. The education of the (child) _____ started when they
8

were (baby) _____ . Learning usually involved sitting still, listening
9

intently, and waiting but not asking (question) _____ . Thus, the
10

(learner) _____ could have many (experience) _____ in
11   12

their (life) _____ rather than just listening to information from
13

(other) _____ . In addition, they also heard many (story)
14

_____ because of the importance of knowledge through oral
15

tradition in those (culture) _____ .
16

Activity 2

Find seven mistakes in nouns in the following paragraph.

Storytelling was one important part of educating members of a tribe by passing on both informations and customs. This kind of educations relied on the memorys of the storytellers of each generation. The tribes learned about many important event in the history of their people as well as some important values. Storytelling was one particular ways of preserving the society's beliefs and observances and making sure they flourished. Ceremonys, dances, and prayers were created from the knowledges gained from these stories.

Activity 3

A. Fill in the blanks of the following student journal entry with the correct form of the nouns from the list below. Be sure to make the noun plural for the sentence if necessary. Use each noun only one time.

topic	assignment	homework	society
	family	information	example	

Today in our cross-cultural class we learned about the

different way of life of several _____ . The most
                                        1

interesting _____ for me was the idea of
                    2

extended _____ . At the end of class our
                3

teacher gave us a lot of _____ to complete,
                                    4

including three _____ . One of them is to write
                        5

some personal _____ about how we grew up
                        6

and whether or not we had an extended or nuclear family.

We also need to give some specific _____ .
                                            7

B. *Following is the student's response to the homework assignment mentioned in part A. Fill in the blank spaces with the correct form of the noun and circle the correct verb or auxiliary to fit the sentence.*

I grew up in and still live in an extended family _____ .

                                      medicine

1. I grew up in and still live in an extended family _____ . Three
   of my _____ (has/have) always lived near me, so I see them at

(1) situation

(2) grandparent
   least once or twice a _____ . My uncle and aunt (rent/rents) a

(3) week
   _____ next door to ours. They have a _____ and two

(4) house

(5) son
   _____ , and we (has/have) always attended the same schools.

(6) daughter

2. My grandmother is always there to take care of me. She says that
   _____ (are/is) the most important thing in life, so she often

(1) health
   prepares _____ and home _____ for me when I am

(2) food

(3) remedy
   sick. For example, if I have a _____ , she prepares her home-

(4) cold
   made chicken _____ , and when I have a stomach

(5) soup
   _____ , she makes her special _____ for rice. She tells

(6) problem

(7) recipe
   me that rice (is/are) always good for you. Her folk _____ always

(8) medicine
   (help/helps) me too.

3. My cousins and I like to complete our _____ together.

(1) homework
   Mathematics (is/are) my most difficult _____ , so my cousin

(2) subject
   (work/works) with me, especially when we have a _____ . She

(3) test
   is very strong in math and science, but I have a lot of _____

(4) trouble
   with those subjects. I guess _____ (are/is) on my side because I

(5) luck
   have such a close _____ to help me all the time.

(6) family

4. Communication in my family (is/are) very important and we make sure
   to spend _____ together. In the evening, we often all sit

(1) time
   around the kitchen, drinking a lot of _____ and _____

(2) tea

(3) coffee
   and sharing _____ . Sometimes we also talk about our

(4) story
   _____ and give each other _____ , which (is/are)

(5) problem

(6) advice
   almost always helpful.

Presentation 2
Quantifiers with Count/Non-Count Nouns

Some **people** have **many relatives** in large extended families. In these families, children may have **a great deal of communication** with their different family members.

Questions

1. Look at the nouns in bold and label each one as count or non-count.

2. Circle the word in bold before each of these nouns. What are the rules for using these words?

Explanation—Quantifiers

1. Words of quantity (quantifiers) tell us *how much*. There are several words or expressions of indefinite quantity that we use with nouns. Some of these words/expressions may be used with count and non-count nouns, and others may be used with only one type of noun.

2. Following is a chart of some common quantifiers to use with nouns.

Countable Only	Uncountable Only	Both Countable and Uncountable
a couple of	a little	no/any
a few	a great deal of	some
several	much	a lot of/lots of (informal)
many		

Do not use *no* in a negative sentence. Use *any* in negative sentences and questions only. *Much* is usually used only in negative sentences and questions. *A lot of* is more commonly used for affirmative statements.

INCORRECT: My friend doesn't have no family here.

CORRECT: My friend has no family here. My friend doesn't have any family here. Does your friend have any family here?

Practice

Activity 4

Circle the correct word in parentheses.

Native Americans have always spent (a lot of/many) (time/times) teaching

through storytelling. Because they did not have (no/any) written language,

they passed on (a great deal of/many) (knowledges/knowledge) and (much/many) (traditions/tradition) through their stories. They placed

(several/a great deal of) (importances/importance) on these stories for

(several/much) (reasons/reason).

Activity 5

A. Complete the following sentences by choosing one of the quantifiers in parentheses and then adding any information that makes sense. Then write another sentence using a quantifier you did not choose for the first one.

When I was a child, . . .

1. my teachers didn't give us (much/many) _____ .
    _____

2. my parents helped me with (a great deal of/several) _____ .
    _____

3. my friends and I played (a lot of/ a great deal of/a couple of) _____
    _____ .
    _____

4. I enjoyed (a few/a little) _____ .
    _____

B. Write three questions for your partner about education in his/her culture or the place you are both now living. Then write three more questions about family life in your partner's culture or the place you are both now living. In each question use one of the nouns listed below and a quantifier. Then answer your partner's questions using complete sentences. Use a different noun from the list and as many different quantifiers as possible in each sentence.

Nouns				
belief	knowledge	discipline	information	stability
obedience	assignment	observance	homework	health
happiness	fun	source	book	lesson
test (or quiz)	review	exercise	essay	origin
Quantifiers				
a couple of	a few		many	several
a little	a great deal of		much	a lot of

Articles

A/An/The/Zero Article

¹**Rituals** can help **people** find **harmony**. ²A **sandpainting** is **an example** of such **a ritual**. ³**Sandpainters** use **materials** such as **pollen** and **sand** to bring **a sick person** back to **health**. ⁴**The sandpaintings** are meant to restore **the health** of **the sick person**. ⁵**The colors** used in **the paintings** are symbolic.

Presentation

Questions

1. Look at sentences 1 to 3, and circle the words *a* or *an*. Is each of the nouns after these words singular or plural?

2. Look at the bold nouns in sentences 4 and 5. Why do they all have *the* before them?

3. Look at the bold nouns in sentence 1. Why don't they have an *a* or a *the* before them?

Explanation – Articles—Using *a/an*, *the*, or No Article (Zero Article)

When we think about using articles, we have four choices as follows:

a or *an*	*the*	no article
indefinite article	definite article	zero article (0)

We use these according to the noun that follows as the chart below indicates.

indefinite—*a/an/*zero article (general/not a specific noun)	definite—*the* (specific noun/something known or previously identified)
singular count nouns—*a* or *an* *A ritual* can heal *a sick person.*	singular count nouns *The sick person* can heal from this ritual.
plural count nouns—zero article *Rituals* can help *sick people.*	plural count nouns *The sick people* use specific rituals to heal.
non-count nouns—zero article *Pollen* and *sand* can be used in sandpaintings.	non-count nouns *The health* of the sick person is restored.

Indefinite Articles—*(a/an)/*Zero Article

1. Use an indefinite article *(a/an)* for a singular countable noun. It means this noun is not specific but more general. We may use the indefinite article when the listener or speaker is not familiar with or doesn't know the noun (or thing) we are talking about.

    A ritual can help *a sick person. A sandpainting* is an example of *a ritual.*

    IMPORTANT: An indefinite article indicates that there is only one of the item you are talking or writing about. Therefore, we use indefinite articles for singular count nouns *only.* **Do not** use indefinite articles with the following: plural nouns/non-count nouns/most proper names. It may be helpful to think of an indefinite article as the number *one.*

    A ritual (one ritual) can help *a sick person* (one sick person).

2. We use the *an* form of the indefinite article when the following word has a vowel *sound.*

    In *a ceremony, a priest practitioner* might use *an herb* as part of *a ritual.*

    A person with *an illness* might identify with *a hero* in *a song* in order to gain some strength.

    REMEMBER: The *an* goes before a vowel **sound,** not before every vowel. Therefore, sometimes you will find **an** before a consonant because it has a vowel sound *(an herb),* and *a* before a vowel because it has a consonant sound *(a university).*

3. We use an indefinite article when we are talking about something for the first time. When we mention this item again, we use the definite article because it has already been identified. (See page 205 for more information about definite articles.)

    A sandpainting can help heal *a sick person. The sick person* can gain strength from the story that goes with *the sandpainting.*

4. We use no article/zero article (0) when we have a general (indefinite) plural countable noun or a general (indefinite) uncountable noun.

> *Rituals* can help sick *people. Sandpaintings* are used in healing *ceremonies.*
>
> *Pollen* and *sand* are used in *sandpaintings.*

NOTE: A singular count noun must always have some word before it, even if it is not an indefinite article.

CORRECT:	The priest used *a sandpainting* OR *his sandpainting* OR *that sandpainting* to heal the sick person.
INCORRECT:	The priest used sandpainting.

Practice

Activity 1

Circle the correct form of the indefinite article (a/an) *in the following sentences.*

1. (A/an) nuclear family usually consists of (a/an) mother, (a/an) father, and (a/an) child or children. (A/An) extended family includes more people, such as (a/an) grandparent, (a/an) uncle, (a/an) aunt, and (a/an) cousin.

2. Storytelling is (a/an) oral tradition in many places in the world. It is (a/an) important way of teaching part of (a/an) society's history.

3. (A/An) sandpainting is also known as (a/an) dry painting. For the Navajos, it is (a/an) way to heal (a/an) unhealthy person. It is also (a/an) artistic expression of (a/an) song about (a/an) hero.

 ### Activity 2

Fill in each space below with a, an, *or* 0 *(to show no article necessary).*

Native Americans told _____ stories as part of their education
 ₁
system. In telling _____ story, _____ tribe could pass on
 ₂   ₃
_____ sacred information. These stories could provide
 ₄
_____ basic tools and _____ knowledge for
 ₅   ₆
_____ tribe's survival. Through these stories _____
 ₇   ₈
children could learn about _____ important events, such as
 ₉

_____ disaster or _____ calamity that occurred
      10   11

_____ years before. They could also learn the story of
      12

_____ honest person or _____ person of other
      13   14

_____ virtues. _____ obedient child listened to and
      15   16

learned from all of these things.

Activity 3

Find 12 mistakes in the following paragraph. Fix each mistake in one of the following ways:

   a. *Change an incorrect indefinite article (a/an) to the correct indefinite article.*
   b. *Add an indefinite article (a/an) if it is missing.*
   c. *Remove an incorrect indefinite article to make it a zero article.*

Do not change the mistakes in any other way.

An totem pole was another way to tell story. A tribes from the Pacific Northwest used giant cedar trees for these poles. Cedar tree has a strong wood which can be carved easily by a skilled carver. When carvers worked on totem poles, they often made a artistic representation of a animal. They also sometimes made image of a supernatural being. A carvings such as these told the story of a family's history. A skilled carver could become a important member of his society as well as a wealthy person. Usually carvers received their payment in the form of a food and a valuable items.

Definite Article—*the*

1. We can use the definite article *the* before all of the following kinds of nouns:

    • singular countable   • plural countable   • uncountable

    The Navajo tribe has many rituals, including sandpaintings.
    Sandpaintings are used in *the tribe's rituals* to heal sick people.
    The priest practitioner of this tribe conducts *the rituals* to restore *the health* of *the sick person.*

    We use the definite article *(the)* for specific nouns. The listener or reader knows the noun that the speaker or writer is talking about. There are several ways the listener or reader may know this as follows:

    • There is only one of these things in the world: *the Navajo tribe.*

    • There is only one of these things in the specific environment you are talking about: *the priest practitioner*—the only one in the tribe.

- You have already mentioned this item and the reader or listener now knows about it. The Navajos have *a ritual* for sick people. *The ritual* uses a sandpainting for healing.

- You give more information about this noun, so this information makes the noun more specific. The sandpainting ritual restores *the health* of a sick person.

- Certain words tell us the noun is unique or specific: *the first* ritual, *the last* ritual, *the longest* ritual (See Lesson 32, pages 234–235 for more information about superlatives.)

2. Definite articles are also sometimes used in names of specific places or geographical areas.

Use *the*	Do not use *the*
Some countries (usually if plural names): the United States, the Philippines, the Netherlands	Most countries: China, Brazil, Japan, Saudi Arabia, Mexico, Italy
Specific sites/attractions/places to stay in cities: the Metropolitan Opera, the Louvre, the Grand Hotel, the Sports Arena, the Coliseum	Cities, towns, states: London, Seoul, Smalltown, Florida Street and Park Names: Fifth Avenue, Broadway, Central Park
Deserts, island groups, mountain ranges, areas of land or regions: the Sahara, the Seychelles, the Alps, the northwest	Individual islands or mountains: Cuba, Bali, Mt. Everest, Mt. Fuji
Oceans, seas, rivers: the Indian Ocean, the Nile, the Danube, the Red Sea	Individual lakes: Lake Titicaca, Lake Michigan, Lake Victoria

Activity 4

Read the following short conversations. Then answer True (T) or False (F) for the questions that follow each one.

José: For my next vacation I'd like to travel to a new and different country.

Alma: That sounds interesting, but before you go, you should learn something about the customs there.

José: You're right. Maybe I'll get a book and do that after I make my plans.

_____ 1. José knows exactly which country he would like to go to on his next vacation.

_____ 2. Alma thinks José should learn about the specific customs of the place he will visit.

_____ 3. José knows which book he will get before he travels.

Carol: Would you like to see the interesting souvenir I bought on my trip to Vancouver last week?

Mike: Sure. Where is it?

Carol: Right now it's on a table in the living room. I'm going to hang it on the wall with my other carvings soon.

Mike: Did you buy it in a museum shop?

Carol: No, I bought it directly from the artist at an art gallery.

_____ 1. Carol probably bought only one souvenir on her trip to Vancouver.

_____ 2. Carol has one living room and only one table in it.

_____ 3. Carol has a specific wall where she hangs things for display.

_____ 4. Mike thinks there is only one museum shop in Vancouver.

_____ 5. There probably are several art galleries in Vancouver.

Activity 5

A. *Find eight mistakes with articles in the sentences below and show how to correct them.*

1. Native Americans who lived in Pacific Northwest made different kinds of totem poles.

2. Totem pole is a kind of carving.

3. A memorial poles were carved to remember dead chiefs.

4. Chiefs usually used talking stick. They used these sticks to get attention of the people at their gatherings.

5. The Inupaiq people live in Arctic area. Some of them live in the Alaska, but others live in Canada.

6. All the Inupaiq people share a common values and speak the same language.

B. *Circle the correct article or zero article in parentheses.*

(Review subordinating conjunctions: Unit Two, pages 42–49 and relative clauses: Unit Five, pages 144–160.)

For hundreds of years, people who live in (a/an/the) Cochiti Pueblo of
                                         1
(the/0) New Mexico have been making traditional clay pottery of figures of
  2
(a/0) storytellers. More recently, (a/an/the) Cochiti woman reinvented this
  3   4
figurative pottery when she made her first clay storyteller in 1964. This

woman, who was named Helen Cordero, started out by creating (a/an/0)
                                                              5
figures that followed (a/an/the) old tradition. (The/0) traditional ceramic
                         6   7
figure was known as a "singing mother." She changed this figure by

exchanging (a/an/the) mother for (a/an/the) grandfather figure. This new
             8   9
figure was (a/an/the) old man sitting with his mouth open and his eyes
            10
closed while he was telling (a/an/the) story. She also gave (a/an/the)
                              11   12
storyteller many children instead of just one. In her figures (a/an/the)
                                                                13
children were all sitting in (a/an/the) lap of (0/the/a) storyteller or around
                              14   15
him while they were listening to (a/an/the) stories.
                                   16

Activity 6   *(Review relative clauses: Unit Five, pages 144–160.)*

Fill in the spaces below with one of the following: a, an, the, 0 (zero article).

In _____ Southwestern area of _____ United States
        1   2
there is _____ group of Native Americans called _____
                3   4
Pueblo people or _____ village dwellers. Among this group of
                        5
people are _____ Hopi, who live in _____ small area of
                  6   7
_____ Arizona. _____ Hopi people have _____
        8   9   10
unique artistic expression of their culture called *katsina* or *tihu carvings.*

These are _____ artifacts that reflect their cultural and religious
                 11
traditions.

_____ *tihu* carving is _____ small, brightly painted
        12   13
wooden figure and each one represents _____ important
                                              14
benevolent spirit being in Hopi culture. _____ exact number of
                                                 15
these spirit beings (called Katsinam) is not known, but there are probably

between 250 and 500 of them, and each one can be represented by

_____ different *tihu.* In _____ Hopi stories these Katsinam
        16   17

normally live in _____ San Francisco Mountains near
                        18

_____ Grand Canyon. The tihu help teach _____ children
      19   20

in this tribe _____ stories and _____ traditions that have
                    21   22

remained with these people for generations. Each one is also _____
                                                                      23

example of artistic skill and craftsmanship that continue to be part of

_____ lives and traditions of these people.
      24

Activity 7

Think of some traditional handmade artifacts or other traditional objects from your culture. These may be things made by artists, or they may be other traditional objects/artifacts used for important days or at specific rituals or ceremonies. They might be a kind of clothing or an everyday object.

Write at least five sentences to describe one of these objects. Answer as many of the questions below as you can in your sentences.

1. What is the name of this object/artifact?

2. Where is this artifact/object traditionally found?

3. Who makes this object/artifact?

4. What is this object/artifact made from? Do you know how it is made?

5. How old is it? For how long have people in your culture been using it?

6. What is it used for?

7. Why is it important in your culture?

_____

_____

_____

_____

_____

INTRODUCTION TO PREPOSITIONS

1. What is a preposition?

   A. There are many prepositions in English, such as *in, at, on, to, from,* etc. These words show a relationship between the nouns and pronouns that follow them and other parts of a sentence.

   B. Prepositions and the words that follow them are called *prepositional phrases.*

   EXAMPLE:

   My friend lives <u>on the Hopi reservation</u> <u>in Arizona</u>.
                preposition   prepositional phrase

2. Look at the following sentence, which is missing prepositions and shows the nouns in bold.

   Jordan gave **a book Susan the library 4 p.m. her birthday.**

   - Which noun is the subject of this sentence? How do you know this? (See Lesson 21, pages 153–154 for review.)
     The subject of this sentence is *Jordan*. We know this because Jordan made the action (gave) and because he is in subject position to the left of the verb.
   - Does this sentence have an object? (See page 154 for review.)
     The object of this sentence is *a book*. We know this because the book received the action; it is what Jordan gave. It is also in object position to the right of the verb.
   - What is the relationship of the other nouns to the other words in this sentence?
     We cannot be sure about the relationship of the other nouns in the sentence to the other words. We need prepositions to tell us these relationships. However, we do not need a preposition to tell us *Jordan* is the subject and *book* is the object.

3. Now look at the same sentence with possible prepositions added in bold. Notice how different prepositions show different kinds of relationships.

   Jordan gave a book **to** Susan **in/near/at/next** to the library **at/before/after** 4 p.m. **on/for** her birthday.

All of the prepositions before the library are about place, but each one says something different about place. All of the prepositions before *4 p.m.* are about time, but each one says something different about time. The prepositions before *her birthday* have very different meanings: one indicates time and the other shows reason. This is why it is important to know how to choose the right preposition for the meaning you want.

4. You learned about subjects and objects in Unit 4, Lesson 21 of this text and reviewed this in preceding item 2. Subjects and objects often have a specific place next to the verb in a sentence, and they do not usually have prepositions before them. However, sometimes prepositional phrases can move around in a sentence because they don't always have a special place.

EXAMPLES:

Jordan gave a book to Susan in the library at 4 p.m. for her birthday.
   S   V   O

In the library at 4 p.m. Jordan gave a book to Susan for her birthday.
                      S   V   O

On her birthday Jordan gave a book to Susan in the library at 4 p.m.
            S   V   O

Remember, although the prepositional phrases may move around, we usually keep the subject—verb—object words next to each other in that order.

INCORRECT:

Jordan in class at 4 p.m. gave to Susan for her birthday a book.
  S   V   O

INCORRECT:

In class at 4 p.m. gave Jordan a book to Susan for her birthday.
               V   S   O

Prepositions of Location

Time and Place

¹Next summer Jason will take a research trip **from** June **to** August so that he can study native cultures **in** the United States. ²He will leave **on** June 1st, but he is not sure exactly when he will return **in** August. ³He is going to travel **from** Southern California **to** Arizona **in** June and then **through** New Mexico and Utah. ⁴He might stay **in** some cities along the way, but he hopes to stay **on** some tribal reservations **between** the larger cities.

Presentation

Questions

1. Underline each of the prepositional phrases that begins with a preposition in bold in the sentences to the left.

2. What is the meaning of each of the bold words? What relationship does each of these words show between the nouns that follow them and the rest of the sentence?

Explanation—Time and Place Prepositions: *to/from/in/on/at/between*

1. Two common prepositions of time and place are *from* and *to*.
    From tells you the beginning time or place. It can also be called the source.
    To tells you the *end* time or place. It can also be called the goal.

    Jason will make a research trip *from* June *to* August.
                                     beginning   end

    He is going to travel *from* New Mexico *to* North Dakota.
                                source   goal

2. *In, on,* and *at* are three other common prepositions of time and place. Often *at* is the most specific and *in* is the most general of these.

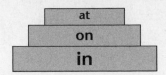

Jason starts his trip *at* 9:30 a.m. tomorrow morning. (exact/specific time)

He is leaving his cat *at* his friend's house. His friend lives *at* 56 Oak Street. (specific place/address)

He is starting his trip *on* Wednesday. (day of the week)

He expects to leave *on* June 2nd. (date)

His first stop might be *on* Main Street to get some new maps. (street name)

He'll probably reach Santa Fe *in* the afternoon. (time of day)

He is taking this trip *in* the summer. (time of year)

The last time he visited Santa Fe was *in* 2002. (year)

He'll stay *in* Santa Fe one day only. (city)

He always does his research *in* the United States. (country)

He usually studies native cultures *in* North America only. (larger area)

NOTE: Use *in* for times of day such as *in* the morning, *in* the afternoon, and *in* the evening, but say *at* night.

3. *In* and *on* can also be used for the following meanings:

in = inside	Jason will stay *in* many hotels.
on = on top of/on the surface of	He will travel *on* some highways and *on* some dirt roads.

Sometimes we will use these prepositions with specific kinds of transportation as follows:

in   car/taxi

on   airplane/train/bus/motorcycle/bicycle

He was riding *in* his car on a highway when he saw some friends *on* a bus.

4. Two other common prepositions that are used for both time and place are *between* and *through.*

between = within two limits of time or two places

He will make several stops *between* those places.

He may arrive *between* 9:00 and 9:30 p.m.

through = from one end to another in time or place/in one side and out another in place

He stayed at the hotel *through* the end of the week. He had trouble going *through* the doorway with his large package.

Review of Other Time Prepositions:
for/since/before/after/until/during

1. In Lesson 10 (pages 65–66) you learned about using *for* and *since* with present perfect verbs when talking about things that happened from the past to the present.

   for = amount of time/   since = start time/
      duration   when the action or situation began

   Jason has been traveling *for two weeks*.
                              prepositional phrase (duration)

   He has been staying in Santa Fe *since yesterday*.
                                   prepositional phrase (start time)

   Sometimes you will also find the preposition *for* meaning duration with other time frames.

   Jason was studying artifacts at a museum *for three hours today*.

2. In Unit Two of *Destinations 2: Writing for Academic Success* (pages 42–49), you learned about subordinating conjunctions of time. Some of these connectors can also be used as prepositions.

   before   Jason arrived in Santa Fe *before the end* of the day.
                                        preposition   noun

             Jason arrived in Santa Fe *before he ate* dinner yesterday.
                                        conjunction S   V

   after   He will go to Colorado *after his stay* in Santa Fe.
                                     preposition   noun

             He will go to Colorado *after he finishes* his visit in Santa Fe.
                                     conjunction S   V

   until   He will stay in Santa Fe *until tomorrow*.
                                       preposition noun

             He will stay in Santa Fe *until he finishes* all his work there.
                                       conjunction S   V

   since   He has been staying in Santa Fe *since last Tuesday*.
                                             preposition   noun

             He has been staying in Santa Fe *since he arrived* there
             last night.   conjunction S   V

3. The preposition *during* means at that time. Do not try to use this word as a connector. Use the conjunction *while* instead.
   (Review the note about subordinating conjunctions: Unit Two, page 45, item 7.)

   During his stay in Santa Fe, he visited two museums.
   preposition   noun

   While he stayed in Santa Fe, he visited two museums.
   conjunction S   V

   INCORRECT: During he stayed in Santa Fe, he visited two museums.

Practice

Activity 1   *(Review conjunctions: Unit One, pages 8–13 and Unit Two, pages 42–49, as well as relative clauses: Unit Five, pages 144–160.)*

A. *Circle each preposition of time or place and underline the prepositional phrase. Indicate whether the preposition is showing a time (T) or place (P) relationship above the preposition. Remember, sentences can have more than one prepositional phrase.*

                                                        P

    EXAMPLE: Several Pueblo tribes are ⓘⓝ New Mexico.

1. The Hopi reservation is located in Arizona and has three mesas.

2. Some Hopi people live at the top of First Mesa in a village called Walpi.

3. On Third Mesa there is a village called Old Oraibi, which may be the oldest continuously inhabited village in the United States.

4. People have been living in Old Oraibi since 1100, yet not all the structures (buildings) have been preserved for all those years.

5. Approximately 100 miles from the Hopi reservation you can find the San Francisco peaks.

6. The Hopis consider these peaks sacred, and several times a year priests travel from the Hopi villages to shrines on the peaks.

7. The Hopis welcomed visitors to their villages until people began to disrespect the laws and customs.

8. Today visitors are welcome, but they must be careful to follow all rules and customs from the time they arrive until their departure from the reservation.

B. *Circle the correct preposition in parentheses.*

1. Jason drove (between/through) the Hopi reservation (during/while) his trip (on/in) July.

2. He started (for/at) First Mesa and then traveled (from/to) there (from/to) Second Mesa (in/on) a few hours.

3. He stopped (on/at) the Visitor's Center (in/on) Second Mesa (on/at) July 15th.

4. He stayed (at/on) the hotel there (between/for) two days (during/until) July 17th.

5. He did not stop (on/at) any shops or souvenir stands (in/on) the highways (between/through) the mesas (on/in) the reservation.

Activity 2   (*Review conjunctions: Unit One, pages 8–13 and Unit Two, pages 42–49, as well as transitions: pages 77–85.*)

A. *Fill each space with any of the following prepositions:* for, at, in, during, to, on, after, from, *or* through. *You may use some words more than one time, but be sure to use each word at least once.*

Jason's mother, Ann, has a large extended family, and all her relatives

live _____ different cities. Every year they all get together
            1

_____ Ann's house _____ a Sunday _____ July.
        2   3   4

They always do this _____ the summer _____ the school
                            5   6

year ends, and this way everyone can easily attend. Everyone arrives

_____ the early morning, so they can spend the entire day there.
        7

Her cousins, aunts, and uncles drive _____ their homes
                                            8

_____ her house. Some have to travel _____ several
        9   10

highways and _____ two or three states _____ over two
                    11   12

hours. However, her grandparents always come _____ an airplane
                                                    13

because they live _____ another state far away, and the driving is
                        14

difficult. Ann's family has been making these get-togethers _____
                                                                    15

many years now.

B. *Follow the same directions as above, using* since, before, through, from, to, in, on, *or* at.

Jason's father, Joe, has a small nuclear family, and they all live _____
                                                                        1

the same town; in fact, they have all been neighbors _____ 1999.
                                                            2

Joe's parents live _____ 63 Oak Street, and his sister's family lives
                        3

_____ the same street just one block away. His brother lives
        4

_____ another neighborhood, but he can easily walk
        5

_____ his apartment _____ his parents' house. He enjoys
        6   7

this walk because it takes him _____ a beautiful park, and he can
                                    8

walk _____ the grass or _____ dirt paths. He can also
            9   10

make the trip more quickly _____ his bicycle. Last week he left his
                                11

house _____ 6 o'clock _____ the evening, and he arrived
            12   13

home _____ the news was finished _____ 6:30 p.m.
            14   15

Joe's family will probably continue to live _____ this town
                                                16

_____ a long time.
        17

Activity 3 *(Review conjunctions: Unit One, pages 8–13 and Unit Two, pages 42–49, as well as relative clauses: Unit Five, pages 144–160.)*

Below you will find two of Jason's journal entries, but all of the prepositions in bold are incorrect. Replace each one with one of the words on the list given. There may be more than one correct answer, but be sure to use each preposition at least once.

A. *for   at   in   on   through*

For First Mesa I walked **on** the village of Walpi. **On** one house
a man was standing **through** the doorway, and he invited me
to see the kachinas that he had just carved. There were two
freshly painted carvings **from** a table **to** the middle of the
room. We talked **from** about ten minutes, but I had to leave
because it was getting late. I did not want to drive my car **in**
night **at** unfamiliar roads.

B. *for   between   from   through   on   until   during   after   to   at   in*

At Friday, I arrived **for** Third Mesa **at** a short drive **to** Second
Mesa **from** Old Oraibi. **From** my drive **on** the two mesas, I
found a place to stop and sit quietly **during** a while. I sat
there and listened intently to try to learn more about
life **through** this place. At first, I heard only some birds
flying **to** tree **from** tree. When I listened more closely, I
could hear the wind **at** the air. Then, **on** a little while I was
able to hear what sounded like small animals running
between some grass. I stayed at this spot **at** late **on** the
morning.

Activity 4

Look at the following announcement of a Native American gathering called a pow wow. Write at least five sentences explaining when and where this pow wow will take place as well as details about the schedule. An example sentence has been given.

EXAMPLE:

There will be a pow wow in Santa Fe, New Mexico.

_____

_____

_____

_____

_____

_____

Other Common Prepositions

For/With/By/Of

[1] Traditionally in the United States the parents **of** the bride make the arrangements **for** their daughter's wedding. [2] In other places, these arrangements may be made **by** the groom and his family. [3] These days when the bride and groom are no longer living **with** their parents, the couple may make the wedding plans **by** themselves.

Presentation

Questions

1. Underline the prepositions in bold and the phrases that follow them in the caption.

2. Do you know the meanings of any of these prepositions?

Explanation—Prepositions—*for/with/by/of*

1. In Lesson 29 (page 213) you learned about prepositions of location (time and place). Four other common prepositions in English are:

   for   *with*   *by*   *of*

2. Two common meanings for the preposition *for* are:

   for = purpose
   The bride's parents make the arrangements *for* their daughter's wedding.

   for = help or benefit for someone else
   The bridegroom bought a wedding present *for* the bride.

3. Two common meanings for the preposition *with* are:

> with = people do something together
> Sometimes the bride and groom are no longer living *with* their parents.

> with = using an instrument or tool to help someone do something
> The bride bought her wedding gown *with* her credit card.

4. In Unit 4 in this text you learned about passive sentences and using *by* with the agent.

> Wedding arrangements may be made *by* the groom and his family.

5. The preposition *by* also indicates the method or how something is done.

> The bride did not order her gown from a store. She made it *by* hand.

> You will often see *by* with types of transportation.

> The couple went *by* limousine to the airport.

6. The preposition *of* can have different meanings. Sometimes *of* can show possession as follows:

> The parents *of* the bride make the wedding arrangements.
> They were married at the home *of* the bride's family.

> Sometimes *of* can indicate a material or substance.

> The bride wore a gown *of* ivory satin.

Practice

Activity 1

Circle the correct preposition in parentheses.

Mr. and Mrs. George Simpson are happy to announce the marriage (of/for)
[1]
their daughter Ann to Mr. David Graves. The couple had a small church
wedding on January 5, 2006 (by/with) about 50 people in attendance. The
[2]
bride wore a silk dress (for/with) a crown (by/of) flowers. The party was at
[3]   [4]
the summer home (with/of) a friend. Friends decorated the house (by/with)
[5]   [6]
balloons and flowers, and other decorations were made (with/by) hand
[7]
(by/of) the bride's mother, who is an interior decorator. Some guests also
[8]
brought food (with/for) the party. The bride's sister baked a large chocolate
[9]
wedding cake (by/with) herself. (By/For) their honeymoon the couple went
[10]   [11]
(by/with) car to Las Vegas.
[12]

Activity 2

Choose a different prepositional phrase from the list below for each space.

a. of the couple   f. of the bride
b. with a diamond ring   g. for his future bride
c. of their parents   h. with the groom's parents
d. by the parents   i. for their children
e. for permission

1. In some cultures a marriage is arranged _____ .

2. Of course, parents want the best match _____ , and the

    children usually obediently follow the decision _____ .

3. In other cultures deciding to marry is the decision _____ .

4. Sometimes the man asks the father _____ to marry his
    daughter.

5. Sometimes the man brings a gift _____ .

6. In some places the couple becomes engaged _____ .

7. Sometimes the parents _____ plan the

    wedding _____ .

Activity 3

Fill in each space below with any of the following prepositions: by, with, for, *or* of.

A. Native American ceremonies _____ marriage vary from tribe to

    tribe. Traditionally, marriage was considered sacred _____

    Native Americans, and divorces or even separations _____

    married couples were rare. Some types _____ observances are

    typically followed _____ different tribes, but other customs

    may be unique. One common ritual often involves the use

    _____ water as a symbol of cleansing or purifying. Larger

    ceremonies _____ big feasts may be typical for some tribes but

    not all. Today some people continue to get married _____

    following some of the traditional customs and rituals.

B. Singing _____ the accompaniment of musical instruments is
    1

    typical at Native American weddings. Sometimes love songs are played

    _____ musicians _____ flutes that are made
    2   3

    _____ cedar wood. Other instruments _____ these
    4   5

    ceremonies may be drums, rattles, and whistles.

C. In the past invitations to wedding ceremonies were often made

    _____ word _____ mouth. Some tribes had smaller
    1   2

    ceremonies and celebrations _____ only a few people. Other
    3

    tribes made large celebrations _____ inviting all members
    4

    _____ the extended families.
    5

Activity 4

*Find five mistakes in each paragraph below and correct each one using the fol-
lowing prepositions only: for, by, with, or of.*

A. Clothing for marriage ceremonies was often made with hand.

    Sometimes these clothes were woven of the groom and other men in

    the village. These outfits were made by different materials, depending

    on where the couple lived and what was available there. For example,

    some brides may have worn long dresses decorated for beads and shoes

    (called moccasins) made for leather.

B. In some tribes, after the wedding the couple lived of themselves, but in

    other tribes they lived for family. The groom often went to live in the

    lodging by the bride's family. He then had to provide food and

    protection of his new wife and family. Sometimes a new place to live

    was built of the newlyweds by their kin.

Activity 5

Write sentences about a wedding using the words given in parentheses. You will need to unscramble the order of the words. Add one or more of these prepositions: with, by, for, *and* of *to each sentence you write.*

EXAMPLE:

The brother of the bride came with his wife and three children.

(his wife and three children/the brother/the bride/came)

1. _____

_____

(the couple/many friends/invited/the groom/the parents)

2. _____

_____

(danced/the bride/her new father-in-law)

3. _____

_____

(the wedding/rented/several men/tuxedos)

4. _____

_____

(cut/they/the cake/a special wedding knife)

5. _____

_____

(to the party/went/they/horse-drawn carriage)

6. _____

_____

(the bride and groom/presents/bought/each other)

Activity 6

Answer the following questions about your native culture in complete sentences. Be sure to include one of the following prepositions in each of your answers: by, with, for, *or* of. *Read your answers to a partner or to the class.*

1. What kind of ceremony do people usually have when they get married (for example, religious or civil, long or short)?

   _____

   _____

2. Do most people have a large ceremony? Who plans the wedding?

   _____

   _____

3. Do most people have a party after the ceremony? What kind of party is typical? Who pays for the party?

   _____

   _____

4. Are there typical presents for the bride and groom? What are they?

   _____

   _____

5. Is there a typical kind of honeymoon after the wedding?

   _____

   _____

6. Does the bride or groom change her or his name after the wedding?

   _____

   _____

Preposition Review and Deleting For/To

[1]**On** some holidays and other special occasions, people give gifts **to** friends and family. [2]Sometimes they might make a relative a birthday present. [3]Other times they send a friend something **for** a special achievement, such as graduation **from** college.

Presentation

Questions

1. Review the meanings of the prepositions in bold. Then underline the subject and verb in each of the sentences.

2. What is the object in each of these sentences? (What do people give in sentence 1? What do they make in sentence 2? What do they send in sentence 3?)

3. Can you think of any other way to say sentences 2 and 3 using the prepositions *to* and *for*?

Explanation—Prepositions—Deleting *For* and *To*

1. In Lesson 21 (pages 153–155) you learned about typical sentence patterns in English. You learned that often you will find the order of words in an English sentence as follows: subject—verb—object.

   On special occasions *people give gifts* to friends and family.
                         S   V   O

   Sometimes *they* might *make* a birthday *present* for a relative.
                    S   V   O

2. In Lessons 29 and 30 in this text you learned about prepositions and prepositional phrases. You learned how they can show different relationships between nouns or pronouns (not subjects or objects) and the rest of the sentence.

   On special occasions people give gifts to friends and family.
       prepositional phrase   prepositional phrase

> Sometimes they might make a birthday present for a relative.
> prepositional phrase

You also learned that sometimes prepositional phrases can move in a sentence. In this lesson you will review some of the prepositions from the previous lessons. You will also learn how two prepositional phrases can move in a special way.

3. Sometimes prepositional phrases beginning with *for* and *to* can move next to the verb. When you move these phrases, you must delete (remove) the preposition. You can make this change only in the following ways:

   a. to = a living thing receives something

      On special occasions people *give gifts* <u>*to friends and family*</u>.

      On special occasions people *give* <u>*friends and family*</u> *gifts*.

   The words *friends and family* now look like an object because they are next to the verb on the right (in object position). However, we know *friends and family* do not receive the action of the verb *give*. People do not pick up and give friends and family, but they do pick up and give gifts.

   b. for = benefit or help a living thing

      Sometimes they might *make a birthday present* <u>*for a relative*</u>.

      Sometimes they might *make* <u>*a relative*</u> *a birthday present*.

   NOTE: Traditionally you will hear these words or phrases called "indirect objects."

4. You cannot make this change when these two prepositions have other meanings. You cannot change the following:

CORRECT:	Many of his friends came from out-of-town to the party.
INCORRECT:	Many of his friends came the party from out-of town.
CORRECT:	Many people came from out-of-town for his party.
INCORRECT	Many people came his party from out-of-town.

5. You will find this change with a small group of common verbs in English.

bring (for/to)	buy (for)	give (to)	make (for)
offer (to)	order (for)	sell (to)	send (to)
show (to)	take (to/for)	tell (to)	

6. Sometimes a sentence will have a pronoun as an object and one of the prepositional phrases beginning with *for* or *to*. In this case, you *cannot* move the prepositional phrase next to the verb.

   She bought *the present* for her brother. She bought her brother the present.   object/noun

   She bought *it* for her brother. (no change possible)
   object/noun

Practice

Activity 1

A. *When do people celebrate the following holidays or special days in the United States? First give the month and then the exact date if you know it. If you do not know about this holiday, just go to the next one.*

EXAMPLE: In the United States Valentine's day is in February.
It is on February 14th.

New Year's Day	Halloween
Mother's Day	Thanksgiving Day
Father's Day	Independence Day

B. *Do you celebrate these holidays in your native culture? If so, are they on the same dates? On which of these days do people give gifts in the United States and/or in your culture? What kind(s) of gifts are given?*

Activity 2

A. *Find five mistakes with prepositions in each of the following invitations and correct them. There may be more than one way to correct some of them.*

B. *Answer the following questions for each invitation:*

- What is the occasion? (What is the invitation for?)
- Does this occasion require a present? If the answer is yes, what might be a good present to bring?

We invite you to share a special day from our family as we celebrate the Golden Wedding Anniversary on our parents

MR. AND MRS. GORDON SIMPSON

Please join us for a celebration beginning in 7:00 o'clock at the evening for dinner and dancing on the
Lighthouse Restaurant
Harbor Drive
Seattle, Washington

Mr. & Mrs. Paul Harmon
request the pleasure of your company on the wedding reception of their daughter
Susan Jane
and
Mr. Brian Bose
at Sunday, the twenty-fifth of May two thousand and seven on one-thirty for the afternoon in home
5524 Boston Lane
Fort Lauderdale, Florida

Join us in a festive evening as we celebrate the fortieth birthday on
Taylor Hemingway
at Friday, July seventeenth to seven o'clock from midnight at
City Lights Bistro
Chicago
Please RSVP by January 15th
Judy and George Cronin

Activity 3   *(Review conjunctions: Unit One, pages 8–13 and Unit Two, pages 42–49, as well as relative clauses: Unit Five, pages 144–160.)*

Read each of the paragraphs and do the following:

A.   *Step 1. Label the subject, verb, and object (if any) in each clause with the letters S (for subject), V (for verb), and O (for object).*

   Step 2. Find and underline all of the prepositional phrases that begin with for *or* to.

   EXAMPLE:

   Valentine's Day is in February on February 14. People often buy
      S   V   S   V

   their sweethearts presents on this day. Children give small candies
                      O   S   V   O

   <u>to their friends and classmates.</u>

1.   Mother's Day is a special Sunday in the United States. Children often buy their mothers cards and give gifts to them. Sometimes school children make small crafts for their mothers in school. Then they bring them home to their mothers as gifts.

2.   On Halloween many children wear costumes and go trick or treating. Sometimes parents buy the costumes, and sometimes they make them for their children. Many children show their costumes to all of their friends. Usually children go to their neighbors' houses, and the neighbors give the children candy or pennies.

3.   Gift-giving traditions for marriages varied from tribe to tribe among Native Americans. In some tribes the groom brought the bride's family a dowry. In other tribes the bride and groom made small gift baskets for each other. Sometimes the families of the bride and groom exchanged gifts with each other. In other cases the bride and groom even made gifts for their guests.

4.   The Native Americans of the Pacific Northwest often held *potlatches,* which were large social gatherings with guests from different tribes. These gatherings were given for an important family event or to show someone's status in the tribe. In the past when a family leader gave a potlatch, he sent an invitation to guests through a messenger. If an invitation was accepted, the chief of the invited tribe offered the potlatch host a gift. At the potlatch the host gave gifts to his guests in addition to sharing food.

B. *Read the paragraphs in part A again. If possible, change the prepositional phrases with* for *or* to *by moving them next to the verb and deleting the preposition.*

EXAMPLE:

Children give small candies *to their friends and classmates.*

Children give their *friends and classmates* small candies.

C. *Circle any phrases next to the verb that came from prepositional phrases with* for *and* to.

EXAMPLE:

People often buy (their sweethearts) presents on this day.

Activity 4

What do you do for the following situations, or how do you celebrate them both in your culture and the place you are now living? Do you buy a present for someone on these occasions?

> • Your sister just had a baby.
> • Your best friend just moved into a new house.
> • You are going to a friend's house for dinner tonight.
> • Today is your last day of school, and you want to do something special for a classmate or teacher.

A. *Answer the above questions by writing two or three sentences. In some of your sentences use the prepositions* for *and* to *and some of the following verbs:* bring, buy, give, make, show, tell, offer, *and* send.

_____

_____

_____

B. *Write some of your sentences by moving prepositional phrases with* for *or* to *next to the verb.*

EXAMPLE:

Today is Mother's Day.

I buy a card for my mother. I buy my mother a card.

I take my mother to a nice restaurant for dinner. (no change possible)

_____

_____

_____

Activity 5

Choose a holiday or special day from your native culture that includes gift giving. Write a description of this day by answering the following questions. Be sure to write at least five sentences and to use the prepositions practiced in this unit as much as possible. Write at least one sentence that has a prepositional phrase that you moved next to the verb.

- When is this special day or holiday? What is the exact date?
- Why is this day important?
- What special activities take place on this day? (How do people celebrate this day?)
- What kind(s) of gifts do people give on this day?

_____

_____

_____

_____

_____

Adjectives

Comparatives/Superlatives/Equatives

Presentation

Questions

1. What kind of words are in bold in sentence 1? What kind of word follows *large* and what kind precedes *easy* in that sentence?

2. In sentence 2 what ending do the first two bold words have? What does this ending mean? What word comes before the last bold word in this sentence? Why do the bold words have different forms?

3. In sentence 3 what ending does the first bold word have? What does this ending mean? What word comes before the second bold word in this sentence? Why do the bold words have different forms?

4. In sentence 4, what words are in bold besides the adjectives? What do these words mean?

[1]Some consumers like to shop in **large** chain stores because it is **easy** to find everything they need. [2]Other shoppers prefer **smaller** businesses that often offer **friendlier** service and sometimes **more knowledgeable** salespeople. [3]For some people the Internet provides the **easiest** and **most convenient** shopping experience. [4]Many people think this is **less time-consuming than** shopping in stores, but products online may be **as expensive as** the ones in a store.

Explanation— Adjectives: Comparatives/ Superlatives/Equatives

1. Adjectives describe things, and they can do this in several ways. They may describe color, size, general appearance, or other qualities or characteristics.

   Some consumers like to shop in *large* stores. Shoppers may find *friendly* service in small stores.

If you want to use more than one adjective to describe a noun, follow this order:

number	opinion	size	shape	age	color	noun
one	unusual	large			blue	flower
five	silly			old		songs
two		small	round		red	rocks

2. Adjectives usually come before a noun or after a linking verb. (See Lesson 21 for a review of linking verbs.)

> Some consumers like to shop in *large stores*.
> adjective   noun

> It *is easy* to find everything they need.
> linking verb + adjective

Adjectives in English do not add any endings to agree with nouns. *Do not* add the plural -*s* ending to an adjective.

> Some consumers like to shop in *large stores*.

> Sometimes the service in *small businesses* is better.

3. **Comparatives.** We can use adjectives to compare two people or things to one another.

    a. Short adjectives. Add the -*er* ending to a short adjective (one syllable or two syllables ending in -*y*). For spelling changes see Appendix H, page 267.

    > Other shoppers prefer *smaller* businesses that often offer *friendlier* service.

    b. Long adjectives. For longer adjectives (two syllables or more) you do not add an ending to the word. Instead, you add the word *more* or the word *less* before the adjective.

    > Sometimes a small business has *more knowledgeable* salespeople.

    > Salespeople in a large store may be *less knowledgeable* about some products.

    c. When you mention both things that you are comparing, you also use the word *than*. Be careful not to use *more* with an adjective that is already comparative.

    > CORRECT: The salespeople in that store are *friendlier than* the salespeople in the other store.

    > INCORRECT: The salespeople in that store are *more friendlier* than the salespeople in the other store.

    NOTE: Be careful to spell *than* correctly. Do not confuse it with the word "then" (for time).

4. **Superlatives.** We can also use adjectives to show that something is at the top or bottom of a group of things (more than two things).

    NOTE: You will usually add the definite article *the* before superlative forms.

a. Short adjectives. Add the *-est* ending for short adjectives.

> For some people the Internet provides *the easiest* shopping experience.
>
> That store is far away and is *the least convenient* for me.

b. Long adjectives. For longer adjectives (three syllables or more) do not add an ending to the word. Instead add the word *most* or the word *least* before the adjective.

> For some people the Internet provides *the most convenient* shopping experience.
>
> That store has *the least interesting* selection of jeans.

5. Two common adjectives have irregular comparative and superlative forms as follows:

good   better   best
bad   worse   worst

6. **Equatives.** Equatives follow the pattern *as + adjective + as* and show that two things are equal or the same.

> Some products online may be *as expensive as* the ones in a store.

When you want to show that two things are not the same, you can make the pattern negative: *not as + adjective + as.*

> Sometimes products online are *not as expensive as* the ones in a store.

Practice

Activity 1

Find the adjectives in the sentences and label them as follows: C = comparative, S = superlative, E = equative, or A = adjective (not C, S, or E). The first one has been done as an example.

1. Retailers are very competitive because consumers often look for the
    $\quad\quad\quad\quad\quad\quad$ A

    biggest bargains or the best deals that they can find.
    $\quad$ S $\quad\quad\quad\quad\quad\quad\quad$ S

2. Some small businesses have become more competitive than they were
    in the past because larger businesses have some clear advantages.

3. For example, large stores might offer lower prices than smaller
    competitors for similar products.

4. Sometimes the happiest customers are the people who shop on the
    Internet or through mail-order catalogs because those ways of shopping
    can be so convenient.

5. Products in a catalog may be as cheap as the ones in a store, but there is often an additional charge for shipping. Therefore, the final cost from a catalog may not be as inexpensive as the price of the same item in the store.

6. Smart shoppers can be found everywhere, so the most successful entrepreneurs are usually innovative and attentive to the customers' specific needs.

Activity 2

Use the information below about three restaurants for parts A and B.

Restaurant 1	**Restaurant 2**	**Restaurant 3**
Hours: 　6 a.m. to 3 p.m. breakfast served 　until 11 a.m.	Hours: 　7 a.m. to 10 p.m. breakfast served 　all day early bird dinners 　5 p.m. to 6 p.m.	Hours: 　8 a.m. to 10 p.m. breakfast served 　until noon dinner from 6 p.m.
Dress: casual attire	Dress: casual attire	Dress: casual, dressy 　for dinner

A. *Fill in each space with a comparative or equative form of the adjective in parentheses.*

1. Restaurant 2 opens (late) _____ than restaurant 1.

2. Restaurant 1 stops serving breakfast (early) _____ than restaurant 3.

3. Restaurant 2 stays open for business (late) _____ than restaurant 3.

4. Restaurant 2 probably has a (extensive) _____ menu than restaurant 1.

5. Restaurant 2 offers (economical) _____ dinners than restaurant 3 because restaurant 2 has early bird specials.

B. *Fill in each space with a superlative form of one of the adjectives below. Use a different adjective for each answer.*

formal   extensive   short   expensive   long

1. The restaurant with the _____ hours for breakfast is restaurant 2.

2. Restaurant 1 has the _____ hours of business.

3. Restaurant 1 probably has the _____ menu because it serves only breakfast and lunch.

4. Restaurant 3 has the _____ dress code.

5. We can guess restaurant 3 has the _____ dinners because of its lack of early bird specials.

 Activity 3

Find ten mistakes with comparatives, superlatives, and equatives in the following conversation and show how to correct them.

Shopper: Hello, can you help me? I'm looking for a printer for my digital camera.

Salesclerk: Sure, we carry three kinds. This small one is our bestest and most popular model, but it's also the more expensive.

Shopper: I'm looking for a reliable product. The price is not as important the quality. However, I only have $150, so I can't buy anything at a highest price than that.

Salesclerk: Sorry, this one is expensiver than that, but I can show you another popular one that fits your price limit. This one is almost good as the other model. Biggest difference is that the other model prints higher quality photos that are more larger than 4 × 6.

Shopper: What about this third one?

Salesclerk: That also prints high-quality photos, but it uses ink quickly and you may have to change ink cartridges often. That makes it the more expensive to use of the three models.

Shopper: No, I need something with better value. I'll take the second one you showed me.

Salesclerk: That's a good choice. I think you'll be happiest with this one than the less expensive one.

Activity 4

Imagine you are comparison shopping between the following three ways of buying groceries. Use this information to complete parts A, B, and C below.

Store 1	Store 2	Store 3
large chain grocery store	organic health-food store	Internet grocer
10-minute car ride	5-minute walk from home	shop online at home
$5 delivery charge	free delivery	$5 delivery charge— next day
2-lb. box sugar— $1.99	bulk raw sugar— $1.50 lb.	1-lb. box sugar— $1.29
1 dozen large eggs— $1.89	1 dozen large eggs— $1.89	1 dozen large eggs— $1.99
1 gal. milk—$1.80	1 gal. organic milk—$1.95	1 gal. milk—$1.79

On a separate piece of paper, use the following adjectives to write sentences as instructed below. Use each adjective at least one time.

healthy	convenient	cheap	expensive
close to home	fast	easy	available

A.   Write three sentences that make comparisons between these kinds of shopping.

B.   Write two sentences using equatives about these kinds of shopping.

C.   Write three sentences using superlatives about these kinds of shopping.

Activity 5

Look at the following ways to shop and think about which ones you like to do and which ones you do not like. Write five sentences about your preferences using a comparative, a superlative, or an equative with adjectives in each of your sentences.

large warehouse	Internet shopping	small local store
catalog (mail order)	discount chain store	large department store

Gerunds as Subjects and Objects

[1]**Designing** a profitable small business is often a difficult task. [2]A small business owner should **consider studying** the competition. [3]**Getting** this information often takes some time; however, without this knowledge a new business owner **risks losing** his/her investment.

Presentation

Questions

1. Look at the first word in sentence 1 and sentence 3. Are these words used as subjects, verbs, or objects? How do you know this?

2. Look at the two bold words next to each other in sentences 2 and 3. Which of these words are the verbs?

Explanation—Gerunds as Subjects and Objects

1. A gerund is the *-ing* form of a verb but it acts like a noun in the sentence. It is not the verb of that sentence or clause.

   Designing a profitable small business *is* often a difficult task.
      gerund   verb

   A small business owner should *consider studying* the competition.
                                  verb   gerund

2. A gerund can be a subject of a sentence or clause. When a gerund is a subject, it is always singular, and the verb that follows must also be singular.

   Designing a profitable small business *is* often a difficult task.

   Getting this information often *takes* some time.

   When a subject of a sentence contains two gerunds, the verb is plural.

   Designing and starting a profitable small business *take* time.

3. A gerund can also be an object after certain verbs.

> A small business owner should *consider studying* the competition.
> Without this knowledge a new business owner *risks losing* his/her investment.

Some verbs followed by a gerund are:

advise	discuss	finish	practice	suggest
appreciate	dislike	imagine	quit	support
avoid	enjoy	keep (continue)	recommend	tolerate
celebrate	explain	mind (not like)	regret	understand
consider	feel like	miss	risk	

(For a more complete list of these verbs, see Appendix C, page 264.)

4. Gerunds can also follow the verb *go* when someone is discussing certain activities, in particular enjoyable or recreational activities.

> People often *go shopping* when there are big sales, but sometimes they just *go window shopping.*
> Yesterday I *went hunting* for bargains at several large discount stores.

Practice

Activity 1

Circle the gerund and underline the verb in each clause of the sentences below.

Creating a successful small business is difficult in today's world for several reasons. For one thing, purchasing products in bulk means that larger businesses are able to offer lower prices on many items. In addition, finding loyal customers may be difficult for smaller businesses because many larger companies keep marketing their products to a wide base of potential customers. Furthermore, using the power of the Internet can help consumers find new and improved business models, such as online auctions. These models compete with more traditional businesses, so small business owners might regret ignoring these kinds of competition.

Activity 2

Fill in the spaces with the gerund form of one of the following words. Use each word only one time.

provide	offer	make	follow
compete	receive	reduce	

How can small business owners tolerate _____ with the larger

companies? They probably cannot justify _____ prices because

they don't have the same kind of purchasing power as larger companies.

_____ value-added strategies is often a way to establish loyal

clients. Customers often appreciate _____ value-added services

and may make a commitment to shop at establishments that provide these

services. Value-added business owners propose _____ customers

with great service, fair prices, and innovative products or services. Thus,

_____ people feel good about their experiences with that

company is important. _____ this trend can be very helpful to any

small business owner in today's market.

Activity 3   *(Review sentence combining: Unit One, pages 8–13, Unit Two, pages 42–49, Unit Three, pages 77–85, and Unit Five, pages 144–160.)*

Find 11 mistakes in the following and show how to correct them.

Some successful business owners have suggested to use the following value-added strategies:

1. Meet customers personally allows you to better understand and gauge their needs. This might mean travel around the country, but it is usually worth the effort. Sometimes to use personal shoppers can make a big difference in sales as well.

2. To have knowledgeable employees is another important strategy. For small businesses, this may be a large expense; nevertheless, they shouldn't mind to spend money for something that will attract more customers. Even own a Web-based business does not prohibit provide information to help customers with their decisions.

3. Been flexible and respond to customers' specific needs is also a good
   way to run a business. Some successful business owners recommend
   customize products when clients want something different.

Activity 4

Complete each of the following sentences by restating the same idea as the original sentence. Begin each of your responses with a gerund of one of the words listed. Use each word only one time in your answers.

think	~~start~~	meet	make	work	spend

EXAMPLE:
My marketing consultant said I need another advertising campaign for my business.

My marketing consultant advised *starting a new advertising campaign*

for my business.

1. She also said I should not pay for expensive television advertising anymore.

   She also said I should quit _____ .

2. I have an idea in my head about a customer newsletter for my store.

   I can't help _____ .

3. Maybe I should talk about the newsletter idea with my consultant.

   Maybe I should discuss _____ .

4. I'll say we should talk about this next week.

   I'll recommend _____ .

5. I've already delayed any discussion about new advertising for too long.

   I've already postponed _____ .

Activity 5

Write sentences that give advice to people starting their own businesses. Choose four of the following words and write two complete sentences with each one as follows:

a. *Start a sentence with the word as a gerund.*
b. *Use the word as a verb of a sentence and follow it with a gerund.*

enjoy	celebrate	finish	imagine
prevent	avoid	postpone	

EXAMPLE: understand

a. Understanding the competition is important for any new business owner.
b. I understood feeling anxious when I started my first new business with all my savings.

_____

_____

_____

_____

Gerunds after Prepositions

[1]Some people may want to become entrepreneurs, but they are **nervous about trying** to take the steps to do it. [2]New business owners should not be **afraid of taking** the risk if they plan well and are **capable of spending** all the hours needed. [3]Many people can **succeed in establishing** their own business if they give it a try.

Presentation

Questions

1. Look at the gerunds (-*ing* words) in bold in all three sentences. What kind of word comes just before each of them?

2. Circle the other words that are in bold and come before the gerunds. What kind(s) of words are these?

Explanation—Gerunds after Prepositions

1. As you learned in Unit 5, prepositions are followed by nouns and pronouns. Since gerunds function as nouns, they may follow prepositions.

    They are nervous *about trying* to take the steps to do it.

    Many people can succeed *in establishing* their own business if they give it a try.

2. There are many possible combinations of words or expressions that include prepositions. Many of these are verbs or adjectives followed by a preposition. A few of them are nouns followed by prepositions.

Below is a list of some expressions that follow this pattern:

noun + preposition	adjective + preposition	verb + preposition
no reason for	famous for responsible for	apologize for blame (someone/something) for forgive (someone/something) for thank (someone/something) for get (someone/something) by
the problem with	bored with	
no point in	interested in inexperienced in	believe in succeed in participate in
the problem of	afraid of tired of capable of guilty of	take care of (the)
	nervous about	think about dream about talk about complain about worry about
	good at	insist on work on count on look into advise against

3. There are a few expressions that include the preposition *to* and follow this pattern (preposition + gerund). Do not confuse these with *to* + infinitive.

> be used to   look forward to
> be accustomed to   object to
> be opposed to   resort to

Some people *object to shopping* on the Internet because they are *accustomed to buying* things in person.

Other people are *used to using* the Internet for their shopping and *are not opposed to making* purchases that way.

NOTE: Do not confuse *used to* + verb (for past habitual actions/conditions) with *be used to* + gerund (which means "be accustomed to"). (See Lesson 1, page 7, for a review of *used to* and the past.)

He *used to shop* mostly with credit cards on the Internet, but he stopped doing that because he was getting into too much debt.

At first he was not comfortable buying things on the Internet, but now he *is used to shopping* for many things that way.

Practice

Activity 1

Complete each statement in the column on the left with the correct information in the column on the right.

_____ 1. Large chain stores are often very good

_____ 2. They are able to beat the competition

_____ 3. Some customers take advantage

_____ 4. In fact, some customers look forward

_____ 5. Thus, these kinds of stores can probably count

a. by offering convenient self-service and low prices to their customers.

b. to shopping from their own homes.

c. at attracting and retaining many satisfied customers.

d. on staying very successful in today's competitive market.

e. of ordering products through these stores' catalogs or Web sites.

W

Activity 2   (Review sentence combining: Unit One, pages 8–13, Unit Two, pages 42–49, Unit Three, pages 77–85, and Unit Five, pages 144–160.)

A. Fill in the spaces with one of the expressions below and the gerund form of the word given.

| advised her against | stop her from | inexperienced in |
| had some ideas for | insisted on | famous for |

A few years ago my friend Deborah was young and _____
(1) run
a business; nevertheless, this did not _____ a prosperous
(2) establish
restaurant. She _____ a completely vegetarian menu;
(3) create
however, some of her friends and family _____ that.
(4) do
After she researched competing restaurants and the market in her area, she

_____ the original plan. Today her restaurant is
(5) follow
_____ excellent vegetarian dishes at reasonable prices.
(6) serve

B. *Fill in the spaces with a preposition from the list below and the gerund form of the word in parentheses. Use a different preposition for each answer.*

to	about	of	into	for	by

At first she was faced with the problem (have) _____ almost no

capital to start a restaurant, so she looked (apply) _____ for a bank

loan. She also talked (find) _____ people who had money to

invest. However, she was unable to get enough money (try) _____

these ways. Therefore, she reluctantly resorted (borrow) _____ just

enough money from her family in order to get started. She apologized (ask)

_____ them for this money, but they were happy to help her.

C. *Find six mistakes in the following paragraph and show how to correct them.*

Deborah's restaurant has become one of the most popular establishments

downtown; in fact, some say she is responsible starting an economic revival

of the area. Now she is interested on opening a second restaurant. She

looks forward to become even more successful in the future, and she even

thinks about to open a business school or a consulting agency to help other

small business owners. She never gets tired of work with others, and she tells

them to believe with taking chances in order to establish their own success.

Activity 3

Fill in the spaces below with two words: a preposition and a gerund form of one of the words listed below. Use each word only one time.

try	go	have	shop	take

1. One reason _____ to smaller stores for an important purchase is
    the more personalized service often available.

2. Some customers complain _____ at large stores because they
    prefer getting the better service.

3. They feel there is no point _____ to find something they need if
    no one is available to help them.

4. They object _____ to search for things by themselves.

5. Do you usually insist _____ your business to certain stores?

Activity 4

Continue the following sentences using a preposition and the gerund form of one of the words in parentheses. Use your own ideas to finish the sentences.

EXAMPLE:

Jill likes to shop from catalogs instead (go/spend) _____

Jill likes to shop from catalogs instead *of going to the mall to* _____ *buy things.*

OR   Jill likes to shop from catalogs instead *of spending time at the mall to shop.*

1. Small business owners worry (keep/lose) _____

_____

_____

2. For shopping on the Internet, some people advise (use/go) _____

_____

_____

3. We can thank the Internet (provide/make) _____

_____

_____

4. Today many people are used (shop/buy) _____

_____

_____

5. Some shoppers are not interested (purchase/go) _____

_____

_____

6. Some shoppers are guilty (spend/not pay attention to) _____

_____

_____

Infinitives

Verbs Followed by Gerunds and Infinitives

[1]Some people **want to work** from their own homes, and in today's technological world, many people **manage to participate** in this trend. [2]In some cases companies may **hire people to perform** consultant work; in other cases, telecommunication technology **allows people to conduct** all or most of their business from home. [3]In any case, employers **expect to receive** the same quality of work from any location.

Presentation 1

Questions

1. Look at the bold words in sentences 1 and 3. What words follow the verbs?

2. Look at the bold words in sentence 2. How are these different from the bold words in sentence 1 and sentence 3?

Explanation—Infinitives after Verbs— With and Without Objects

1. Infinitives (*to* + simple form of the verb) follow certain verbs.

    Some people *want to work* from their own homes, and in today's technological world many people *manage to do* this.

    Some verbs followed by an infinitive are:

afford	agree	appear	attempt	can't afford	can't wait
decide	fail	grow	hope	intend	learn
manage	mean	offer	plan	prepare	refuse
request	seem	wait			

    (For a more complete list of these verbs, see Appendix D, page 264.)

2. Some verbs require an object (a noun or pronoun) before the infinitive.

In some cases companies may *hire people to perform* consultant work;
verb   object

in other cases, telecommunication technology *allows people to conduct*
verb   object

all or most of their business from home.

Some verbs followed by an object and infinitive are:

advise	allow	cause	convince	enable	encourage
forbid	force	get	hire	invite	order
permit	persuade	remind	require	teach	tell
urge	warn				

(For a more complete list of these verbs, see Appendix E, page 265.)

3. A few verbs can be followed by an infinitive with or without an object.

ask	choose	expect	help	need	pay
promise	request	want	wish	like	

In any case, employers *expect to receive* the same quality of work from any location.

Employers *expect workers to provide* the same quality of work from any location.

Practice

Activity 1   *(Review conjunctions: Unit One, pages 8–13 and Unit Two, pages 42–49 as well as relative clauses: Unit Five, pages 144–160.)*

Underline the verb + infinitive and circle the verb + object + infinitive combinations in the journal entry below.

After finishing my research for business class, I realized I
would like to start my own consulting firm. I've already
spoken to the professor, and he advised me to be sure I
understand all the steps involved in setting this up. He also
urged me to hire an accountant who can help me with the
financial information. Although starting a small business
may appear to take little effort, that is not true at all. I
think the process of putting all of this together will help me
to learn many things that I can't learn from a textbook or in
a classroom.

Activity 2

A. *Fill in the spaces using all the words in parentheses. The story should be in past time and each answer should include an infinitive. The first one has been done as an example.*

Several months ago Joe Owens (decide/quit) <u>decided to quit</u> his job and work at home. Unfortunately, he (fail/realize) _____ what a difficult
₁
change it could be. For years his office job (force/him/report) _____ to work at 8:00 a.m., take a half hour lunch break, and leave
₂
no earlier than 5:00 p.m. He (choose/leave) _____ that
₃
environment, and he fully (expect/have) _____ very flexible hours
₄
and more time to himself. However, he was completely surprised when he (struggle/keep) _____ his business going by putting in even longer
₅
hours. Many times his wife (remind/him/remember) _____ all the
₆
things he didn't like about the old job because he seemed so discouraged.

B. *Follow the same instructions as above. This time you will need to add an object in some of your answers and make verbs negative where indicated.*

Joe's experience with his new home business (teach/make sure) _____ that he always studies a situation completely before he
₁
jumps into it. In the beginning he (prepare—negative/spend) _____ so many hours trying to establish new clients. Also, he
₂
(plan—negative/work) _____ day and night researching his
₃
competition or setting up lists of potential clients. He also (fail/realize) _____ that trying to design an innovative and profitable business
₄
would be time-consuming. In other words, this new job (require/make) _____ an even bigger commitment to work than he was making
₅
before. Nonetheless, he (promise/give) _____ this new business at
₆
least a full year to prosper.

Activity 3

Restate the ideas and information in the following conversations using the verb given followed by an infinitive in each of your answers. You may have to add objects as well.

EXAMPLE:

Janet: Please send this information to all the employees in our department.

Marilyn: Sure, I'll e-mail it to everyone before the end of the day.

Janet (tell) _told Marilyn to send out some information to everyone in their department._

Marilyn (agree) _agreed to e-mail everyone before the end of the day._

1. Sue: Jim, could you please mail the legal documents through an overnight service right away?

    Jim: Okay, but first I have to finish the last part of this project on the computer.

    Sue (ask) _____

    First Jim (need) _____

2. Bob: Hi Bill. Can you come to dinner for our new clients?

    Bill: I'm not sure if I can come because I have a big report to finish.

    Bob (invite) _____

    Bill (hesitate) _____

3. Barbara: I'm really excited about getting my new computer.

    Sara: I am too. Maybe mine will arrive before the end of the day.

    Barbara (can't wait) _____

    Sara (hope) _____

4. Lisa: Steve, you should really think about using your computer skills to start a new business.

    Steve: I can't do that now. I have to repay some loans to my parents, so I need a steady income.

    Lisa (encourage) _____

    Steve (promise) _____

Presentation 2

More about Gerunds and Infinitives

Ingrid **loves to go** to her job every day at the office, but her husband **loves working** at home.

She **prefers spending** her workday at a large company; however, he **prefers to stay** at home and work by himself.

Ingrid particularly **likes to be** with all the people at her office and meet new clients. On the other hand, her husband **likes being** in a quiet environment for work.

Questions

1. Circle the main verb in each group of boldface words. What kind of word follows the verb in each case?

2. Is there any difference in the meaning depending on whether you use gerunds or infinitives with these verbs?

Explanation—Verbs Followed by Either a Gerund or an Infinitive

1. A small group of verbs can be followed by either a gerund or an infinitive. These verb are:

begin	can't stand	continue	forget	hate	like
love	prefer	remember	start	stop	try

   Ingrid *loves to go* to her job every day at the office, but her husband *loves working* at home.

2. For most of these verbs the meaning stays the same when either a gerund or an infinitive follows. However, a few of these verbs have a change in meaning.

   Stop:
   Ingrid *stopped taking* breaks with her co-workers because she didn't like the smell of their cigarettes. (She did this on a regular basis, but then she stopped, and now she no longer does it.)

   Ingrid *stopped to take* a break with her co-workers because she was tired from working hard all day. (The reason she stopped was to take a break; she stopped her work in order to take a break.)

   Remember:
   Ingrid's husband *remembers buying* a new ink cartridge for his computer, but now he can't find it. (He knows he bought it, and he can see himself buying it in his mind. He remembers making this action.)

   Ingrid's husband *remembered to buy* a new ink cartridge for his computer, so he will not run out of ink tonight. (He bought the ink cartridge; he did not forget to buy it.)

Forget:

Ingrid *forgot to give* her boss an important message, so she sent him an e-mail to tell him. (She did not remember to give the message.)

Ingrid *forgot telling* her boss the message, so he was surprised to see the message in his e-mail. (She forgot that she had already told him. She made the action, but she forgot that she did it.)

Activity 4   *(Review coordinating conjunctions: Unit One, pages 8–13 and subordinating conjunctions: Unit Two, pages 42–49 and Unit Six, pages 182–190.)*

Complete each statement in the column on the left with information in the column on the right. You should use each letter on the right only one time.

_____ 1. Even though John forgot to submit all the necessary papers to start his new business,

_____ 2. Jean remembered filling out the paperwork for overtime,

_____ 3. Although Alice stopped working in the Human Resources Department,

_____ 4. The administrative assistant forgot mailing the package to the customer,

_____ 5. Did Vicky remember to install the new computer software,

_____ 6. Why did Greg stop to get his mail

a. she continued to have lunch with her friends there.

b. or did she forget all about it?

c. when he was late for an important meeting?

d. but her paycheck did not include those hours.

e. so she sent another one the next day.

f. he did not have to pay a late fee.

Activity 5

Circle the correct form in parentheses or the word either *to say both gerund and infinitive are possible.*

1. Bob can't afford (to quit/quitting/either) his job in order to start his own business.

2. His brother challenged (him to start/to start/either) a computer-based business at home.

3. Bob seemed (being/to be/either) interested in leaving his job, but he was very nervous.

4. He plans to just continue (working/to work/either) at his present job and to start (to look/looking/either) for other possibilities in the near future.

5. Maybe he can convince (to help/his brother to help/either) him get the details of starting a business.

6. He never remembers (to ask/asking/either) his brother to do this, although he intends (discussing/to discuss/either) the idea every time he sees him.

Activity 6

Find one mistake with gerunds or infinitives in each sentence and show how to correct all of them. The first one has been done as an example.

1. What are the benefits and problems of ~~work~~ working in a small family-owned business?

2. Some people like working in this environment because they want being with people they feel they can trust.

3. Customers also appreciate to shop in an environment they can trust.

4. Furthermore, in comfortable working conditions, workers might attempt learning more about the products and services.

5. On the other hand, family members might begin argue with each other or have disagreements on the job.

6. In addition, small businesses often offer providing their customers with better service, so workers must try to provide this.

Activity 7

Think about a typical day for you at work or at school. What do you do at those places and how do you interact with your teachers and peers? Write five sentences using one of the verbs below in each sentence. A gerund or infinitive should follow each verb you choose.

ask	prepare	expect	practice
agree	choose	help	plan

1. _____

2. _____

3. _____

4. _____

5. _____

Other Infinitives

Presentation

Questions

1. What kind of word do you see before the infinitives in bold in sentence 1?

2. What is the meaning of the bold words in sentence 2? Do the bold words in sentence 3 have the same meaning? Can we use these two expressions in exactly the same way?

[1]It can be **fun to shop** at a mall with friends, but some people find it **easier** and **cheaper to shop** on the Internet. [2]Some people always check store advertisements **to get** the best prices. [3]They may shop only during sales **in order to save** money.

Explanation—Infinitives after Adjectives and Infinitives of Purpose

1. Sometimes an infinitive follows an adjective.

   It can be *fun to shop* at a mall with friends, but some people find it
        adjective   verb

   easier and *cheaper to shop* on the Internet.
    adjective   adjective   verb

2. The adjectives we use in this way often describe feelings, attitudes, sequence, or order.

   She was *happy to receive* the office supplies so quickly even though she had been the *last to request* them.

3. We also use infinitives to show a reason or purpose for something. In this case the infinitive answers the question *Why?*

    Some people always check store advertisements *to get* the best prices.

    This infinitive is a short form of *in order to.*

    They may shop only during sales *in order to save* money.

    In order to + verb and *to* + verb have the same meaning, and they can usually be used in the same situation. However, you may hear the short version (*to* + verb) more often in conversations and informal situations.

4. You may also see an infinitive at the beginning of a sentence as a short form of *in order to*, especially in instructions about how to do something.

    To buy your new phone on-line, go to the following Web site.

Practice

Activity 1

A. *Fill in the spaces with the adjective and an infinitive from the box. Sometimes more than one infinitive may be correct, but use each infinitive only once.*

try	make	be	have	start	sell	begin

1. Recently I was delighted to learn that it is not (difficult) _____ money at home working on a computer.

2. In fact, just about anyone who is (determined) _____ a business or work for himself can do so on the Internet.

3. Of course an appropriate computer with specific capabilities is (necessary) _____ successful at this.

4. Once you have the equipment in place, you will be (ready) _____ your money-making projects.

5. For example, if you are a writer, you should not be (hesitant) _____ desktop publishing.

6. Also, these days musicians are (fortunate) _____ the ability to record their own CDs with a computer.

7. Then they should be (prepared) _____ these CDs at their concerts or on the Internet.

Activity 2

A. *Complete the following sentences by choosing a reason for these purchases from the list below. Use each reason only one time.*

    a. to update his system
    b. to record some of his original music
    c. to keep his new office looking neat
    d. to take pictures for a photo contest
    e. to make higher quality photos from her digital camera

1. John bought some new computer software _____ .

2. Rachel bought a new printer _____ .

3. Pablo bought a new desk organizer _____ .

4. Lorraine bought a new camera _____ .

5. Greg bought a dozen new CDs _____ .

B. *Choose an appropriate instruction from the list below for each space. Some spaces may have more than one possible answer, but you should use each instruction only one time.*

    a. To speak to a service representative,
    b. To pay by check or money order,
    c. To make a purchase from this catalog,
    d. To pay by credit card,
    e. To debit your checking account,

1. _____ use the enclosed order form.

2. _____ press zero or stay on the line.

3. _____ say or press the account number and expiration date.

4. _____ swipe your card through the machine.

5. _____ send your money to the following address.

Activity 3

Rewrite each of the following sentences by restating the information using an adjective and an infinitive. Do not add any new information. Start each sentence with It.

EXAMPLE:
Finding sales at holiday times is easy.
It is easy to find sales at holiday times.

1. Buying a computer that suits your needs is important.

   _____

2. Keeping your receipt for a return is unnecessary in some stores.

   _____

3. Finding the right job can be difficult for some people.

   _____

4. Getting along with co-workers is usually essential in small businesses.

   _____

5. Quitting a secure job to start a new career is brave.

   _____

Activity 4

Fill in each space with an infinitive of purpose using the verbs listed below. For some of your answers use the long form (in order to + verb), and for other answers use the short form (to + verb). Some sentences may have more than one possible answer, but you should use each verb only one time.

emphasize	provide	make	be	display

Advice for Job Interviews

1. _____ a good first impression, dress in business clothes.

2. Shake hands firmly when you first meet the interviewer _____ your confidence.

3. _____ sure they know all your qualifications, tell them about your education.

4. Tell them about your past jobs _____ them with information about your related experience.

5. Ask questions at the end of the interview _____ your interest in them.

Activity 5

Find 11 mistakes with both gerunds and infinitives in the paragraph below and show how to correct them.

Jenna enjoys to listen to music, so she is always eager to adding to her collection. Sometimes it is hard find new and innovative music, but she always manages locating something. For example, she was the first of her friends to ordered specific songs from an Internet service. She was willing to pay a slightly higher price for getting a better quality version of her favorite music from that site. A few weeks ago she was lucky to getting tickets for a concert of her favorite pop artist, and at the concert she could not resist to buy two new CDs. She even goes to swap meets and garage sales in order search for old classics on vinyl. She never stopped to use her old stereo and still is content listen to her oldies.

Activity 6

Complete the following sentences with information about your school, classes, or job.

1. I started studying English in order to _____ .

2. In my classes (or at work) I am always eager to _____ .

3. In the future, I'll use my English to _____ .

4. To earn more money, _____ .

5. To get a better job _____ .

6. You can find a good job by _____ .

7. Right now I am interested in _____ .

Appendix A

Irregular Verb Forms (Past and Past Participles)

Base	Past	Past Participle
be	was/were	been
beat	beat	beaten
become	became	become
begin	began	begun
bend	bent	bent
bet*	bet	bet
bite	bit	bitten
bleed	bled	bled
blow	blew	blown
break	broke	broken
bring	brought	brought
build	built	built
burst*	burst	burst
buy	bought	bought
catch	caught	caught
choose	chose	chosen
cling	clung	clung
come	came	come
cost*	cost	cost
creep	crept	crept
cut*	cut	cut
dig	dug	dug
do	did	done
draw	drew	drawn
dream	dreamt (or dreamed)	dreamt (or dreamed)
drink	drank	drunk
drive	drove	driven
eat	ate	eaten
fall	fell	fallen
feed	fed	fed
feel	felt	felt
fight	fought	fought
find	found	found
fit*	fit	fit
flee	fled	fled
fly	flew	flown
forget	forgot	forgotten
freeze	froze	frozen
get	got	gotten (British: got)
give	gave	given
go	went	gone
grow	grew	grown

(continued)

* The verbs marked with an asterisk (*) have one form for the base, the past, and the past participle.

Base	Past	Past Participle
hang (an object)	hung	hung
have	had	had
hear	heard	heard
hide	hid	hidden (or hid)
hit*	hit	hit
hold	held	held
hurt*	hurt	hurt
keep	kept	kept
know	knew	known
lay	laid	laid
lead	led	led
leap	leapt	leapt (or leaped)
leave	left	left
lend	lent	lent
let*	let	let
lie	lay	lain
light	lit	lit (or lighted)
lose	lost	lost
make	made	made
mean	meant	meant
meet	met	met
overcome	overcame	overcome
pay	paid	paid
put*	put	put
quit*	quit	quit
read*	read	read
ride	rode	ridden
ring	rang	rung
rise	rose	risen
run	ran	run
say	said	said
see	saw	seen
seek	sought	sought
sell	sold	sold
send	sent	sent
set*	set	set
shake	shook	shaken
shoot	shot	shot
show	showed	shown
shrink	shrank	shrunk
shut*	shut	shut
sing	sang	sung
sit	sat	sat
sleep	slept	slept
slide	slid	slid
slit*	slit	slit
speak	spoke	spoken
speed	sped	sped
spin	spun	spun
spit*	spit/spat	spit/spat
split*	split	split
stand	stood	stood
steal	stole	stolen

(continued)

* The verbs marked with an asterisk (*) have one form for the base, the past, and the past participle.

Base	Past	Past Participle
sting	stung	stung
sweep	swept	swept
swim	swam	swum
swing	swung	swung
take	took	taken
teach	taught	taught
tear	tore	torn
tell	told	told
think	thought	thought
throw	threw	thrown
understand	understood	understood
upset*	upset	upset
wake	woke	woken
wear	wore	worn
weep	wept	wept
win	won	won
write	wrote	written

* The verbs marked with an asterisk (*) have one form for the base, the past, and the past participle.

Appendix B

Stative (Non-Action) Verbs

Emotions	Perceptions/Senses	Possession	Mental States
appreciate	feel	belong	believe
care	hear	have	feel (believe/opinion)
dislike	perceive	own	forget
doubt	see	possess	imagine
envy	smell		know
fear	taste		mean
hate			mind
like			realize
love			recognize
mind			remember
please			suppose
regret			think (believe/opinion)
respect			understand
trust			

Wants/Needs/Preferences	Other	
desire	appear	look
hope	be	owe
need	contain	resemble
prefer	cost	seem
want	equal	sound
	exist	weigh

Appendix C

Verbs Followed by Gerunds (verb + *-ing*)

admit	dislike	keep (continue)	quit
advise	enjoy	mention	recommend
appreciate	explain	mind (not like)	regret
avoid	feel like	miss	resist
can't help	finish	postpone	risk
celebrate	forgive	practice	suggest
consider	give up	prevent	support
delay	imagine	prohibit	tolerate
deny	justify	propose	understand
discuss			

Appendix D

Verbs Followed by Infinitives (*to* + base/simple form of verb)

afford	consent	learn	refuse
agree	decide	manage	request
appear	expect	mean	seek
arrange	fail	need	seem
ask	grow	offer	struggle
attempt	help	plan	wait
beg	hesitate	prepare	want
can't afford	hope	pretend	wish
can't wait	hurry	promise	would like
choose	intend		

Appendix E

Verbs Followed by Object + Infinitive*

advise	encourage	need	require
allow	expect	order	teach
ask	forbid	pay	tell
beg	force	permit	urge
cause	get	persuade	want
challenge	help	promise	warn
choose	hire	remind	wish
convince	invite	request	would like
enable			

*Note that many of the words on this list also appear on the previous list. These words may be used with or without objects, depending on the context.

Appendix F

Verbs Followed by Either Gerunds or Infinitives

begin	continue	hate	love	remember	stop
can't stand	forget	like	prefer	start	try

Appendix G

Verb Spelling Changes—Spelling Rules for Adding *-ed/-s/-ing* to Verbs

1. Spelling changes with base + *-ed* form.

    *   If the base ends in *y* and the letter before it is a consonant, replace the *y* with *i* and then add *-ed*.

study	studied	hurry	hurried

    *   For one syllable words: If the base ends in a single consonant preceded by a single vowel, double the consonant before adding *-ed*.

stop	stopped	hug	hugged

    *   For words with more than one syllable: If the base ends in a single consonant preceded by a single vowel and the last syllable is stressed, double the consonant before adding *-ed*.

control/controlled	occur/occurred	prefer/preferred

    *   If the base ends in *e* add *d*.

name	named	smile	smiled

2. Spelling changes with base + *-s* form.

    *   If the base form of the verb ends in a consonant +*y*, change the *y* to *i* and add *-es* for the base + *-s* form.

We study English	He studies English.
The students carry books.	The student carries books.

    *   If the base ends in *x, s, z, sh,* or *ch,* add *-es* for the base + *-s* form.

We wash in the morning.	He washes in the morning.
They fix cars.	She fixes cars.

    *   If the base ends in *o,* add *-es.*

I go to school.	She goes to school.
We do our homework.	She does her homework.

3. Spelling changes with base + *-ing* form.

- For one-syllable words: If the base ends in a single consonant preceded by a single vowel, double the consonant before adding the *-ing*.

jog/jogging	cut/cutting

- For words with more than one syllable: If the base ends in a single consonant preceded by a single vowel and the last syllable is stressed, double the consonant before adding *-ing*.

forget/forgetting	prefer/preferring

- If the base ends in *e*, drop the *e* before adding *-ing*.

make/making	close/closing

- If the base ends in *ie*, change *ie* to *y* before adding *-ing*.

lie	lying	die	dying

Appendix H

Adjective Spelling Changes—Spelling Rules for Adding Comparative/ Superlative Endings

1. For adjectives ending in a single consonant preceded by a single vowel, double consonant when adding *-er* or *-est*.

big	bigger	biggest

2. For adjectives ending in *-y,* change *y* to *ie* when adding *-er* or *-est*.

early	earlier	earliest
happy	happier	happiest

Appendix I

Noun Spelling Changes— Spelling Rules for Nouns

Regular Plurals of Nouns

1. Add -*es:* nouns that already end in -*s*   class/classes gas/gases
              nouns that end in -*ch, -sh, -x* or -*z* tax/taxes   ash/ashes
              many nouns that end in -*o*   hero/heroes tomato/tomatoes

2. Drop -*y* and add -*ies:*   nouns that end in a consonant (*b, c, d, l, m, p,* etc.)
              followed by -*y.*
              city/cities   story/stories

3. Drop -*f* and add -*ves:*   wife/wives   life/lives

Irregular Plurals of Nouns

1. No -*s* ending:

man	men	mouse	mice
woman	women	foot	feet
child	children	goose	geese
person	people	tooth	teeth

2. No form change (same for singular and plural)

Chinese	antelope
Japanese	deer
Swiss	fish
Vietnamese	sheep
	shrimp

Index

Photo Credits